THE RELUCTANT NEEDLE-WORKER

1.00

BETTY SPELLER

with illustrations by Ian Layzell

THE RELUCTANT

NEEDLE-WORKER

Whittet Books

Measurements

Throughout this book all measurements are given in both metric and Imperial. Follow one system or the other. As these two ways of measuring do not always convert easily it is not advisable to work from one system then the other.

First published 1982

Text © 1982 by Betty Speller
Illustrations © 1982 by Whittet Books Ltd

Whittet Books Ltd, The Oil Mills, Weybridge, Surrey

British Library Cataloguing in Publication Data

Speller, Betty
    The reluctant needle-worker.
    1. Sewing — Amateurs' manuals
    I. Title
    646.2   TT710
    ISBN 0-905483-25-1

CONTENTS

Introduction 7

Equipment 9

Threads and Needles 11

Fabrics 13

Your Sewing Machine 17

Basic Stitches 23

Mending and Patching 27
Wools or Loosely Woven Fabrics 27
Cottons, Lawns or Fine Fabrics 27
Knitted Fabrics 28
Applying a Patch 28
Now Disguising it All 30

Fastenings 35
Hooks and Eyes 35
Hooks and Bars 35
Press Fasteners 36
Velcro 36
Replacing Buttons 37
Buttons for Coats and Heavy Garments 37
Dressweight Buttons 38
Buttons for Shirts and Blouses 38
Covered Buttons 38
Replacing Zips 39
   How to Set About it 39
   Lapped Method 40
   Slot Method 41
   Trouser Zips 41

Repairs to Leather, Suede or Synthetic Skin 45
Equipment 45
Sewing Methods 45
Leather Patches 46

Alterations 49
Shortening a Skirt 50
Lengthening a Skirt 50
Making a Waist Smaller 52
Making a Waistband Smaller 52

Making a Waist Larger 52
Making a Waistband Larger 52

Curtains 57
Before Buying Your Curtaining 57
Lengths Required 57
Preparing to Make Them 57
Simple Unlined Curtains 58
Lining Curtains 59
    Loose Lined 59
    Lining Attached 60
    Lock Stitched Linings 60
    Altering the Length 61

Net Curtains 65
Window Nets 65
Buying Ready-Made 65
Buying Ready-Made and Finishing Them 65
Making Them Completely 65
Floor Length Curtains or Nets 66

Cushions 69
Cushion Pads 69
Plain Cushion Cover 70
Patchwork Cushion Cover 70
Machined Patchwork Cushion Cover 72
Oblong Cushion Cover 72

Loose Covers and Upholstery 75
Loose Covers 75
Cutting Out 75
Upholstery 77
Taking it Apart 77
Putting it Together 77
A Boxed Cushion 78

Makes 83
How to Use These Patterns 83
Waistcoat in Two Sizes 83
Gathered Skirt 86
Loose Fitting Blouse 87
Apron 90
Bag and Headscarf 92

Where to Buy 96

INTRODUCTION

Although you may be convinced that you'll never be an enthusiastic
needle-person, you probably need to know how to do a few basic things —
replacing buttons, taking up hems and making clothes fit, for example.
Especially if you're a man, and subject to heckling cries of 'chauvinist'
when you ask her to sew on a button. Man or woman, you may, for
reasons of economy, want to make the odd cushion, curtains or chair
cover. As this book will explain, they're not too difficult; women may
even feel confident enough to progress to a simple top and skirt, waistcoat or bag. I hope that I'll be able to make your fingers nimble, not
thumbs.

It's a great temptation to do things hurriedly — but that can lead
to disasters. The finished work will have that 'home-made' look, which
will always annoy you. So give yourself plenty of time for the job. Sit
in a good light and sit comfortably. Before you start equip yourself
with a few basic materials of the very best you can afford. Nothing is
more frustrating or off-putting than to find you do not have the essen-
tials to hand when needing to do a repair or some sewing.

THIS BOOK'S GOT
ME IN STITCHES!

EQUIPMENT

Good quality scissors, both dressmaker's and small ones with fine points are worthwhile investments. Buy a variety of needles ranging from 'betweens' (very short ones) and 'sharps' (slightly longer) for fine sewing — more about these on page 11 — to darners, 'crewel' (embroidery ones) and blunt-pointed (tapestry) needles. These will all have their uses at some time or another. Both Milwards and Aero are excellent makes; avoid cheap ones, they will just fray the working thread and break it. The smaller the number of the needle, the larger its size.

A reel of tacking thread is also necessary; it is specially made for the job, being fine and soft, and will not mark the fabric. One reel will last ages. Buy a light colour if possible, for, whereas a light colour will seldom 'run' into a darker fabric, the reverse is always possible.

Finally you will need a tape measure, one with Imperial measurements and metric, both on one side is a good idea, and a good thimble — a cheap one really is false economy as it won't last long.

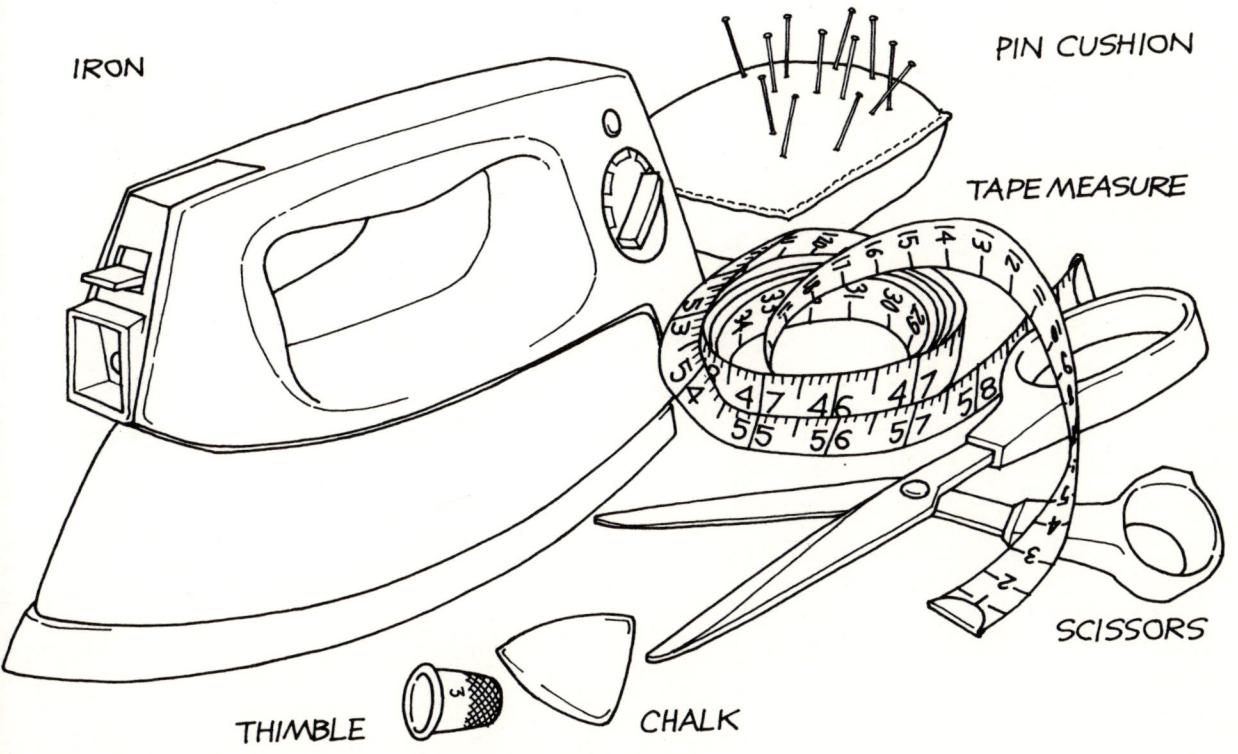

IRON PIN CUSHION TAPE MEASURE SCISSORS THIMBLE CHALK

THREADS AND NEEDLES

Where possible, try to match the kind of thread to the type of fabric you are going to sew. That is to say, use thread of natural fibre (i.e. cotton) for wools, cottons or linens. Use Polycotton (a mixture of Polyester and cotton) for fabrics that are a mixture of synthetic and natural fibres and 100% Polyester thread for completely synthetic fabrics. If in doubt when matching the colour of thread to fabric, choose a darker shade.

Of the natural materials, lightweight fabrics need mercerized cotton no. 60 (the finest) or no. 50 (slightly thicker); for heavier weight, more closely woven fabrics and most woollens, use no. 40. For synthetic and mixture fabrics you will find that generally speaking most manufacturers make only one thickness of Polycotton or Polyester thread, but as this thickness does vary from one make to another, it is as well to shop around and compare the thickness of each before you decide.

For most dressmaking needs, use either betweens or sharps sewing needles. Which one you use just depends on which you find most comfortable to sew with.

Use fine needles for fine fabrics. Lace, lawn, organdie, chiffon, etc., need sizes 8 or 9. Medium-weight fabrics, such as cotton, corduroy dress fabrics or velvet need sizes 7 and 8. Really heavy fabrics such as coatings, denim and furnishing materials, need sizes 5 or 6.

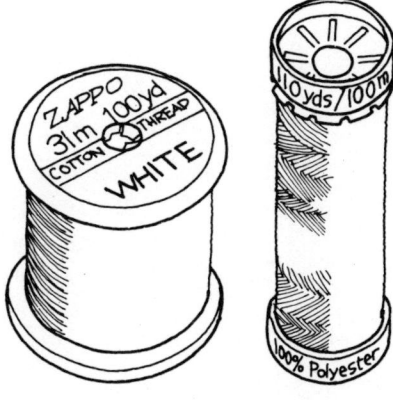

FABRICS

There is a wide selection of fabrics now available and the choice can be confusing. The main thing is to understand the uses of different fabrics - what garments they are suitable for, and which fabrics are difficult to handle and best avoided by the beginner. One or two terms might need explaining:

Selvedges: the firm, finished edges, usually forming a narrow ribbon-like band that run along each side edge of the width of the fabric.

Grain or **nap:** the direction in which the finish of the fabric lies; velvet, corduroy and 'brushed' fabrics all look very different when held with the finish lying in opposite directions. This means that all pattern pieces *must* lie in one direction when you are cutting out a garment and that, you will find, invariably means buying extra fabric. Of course the same applies to print fabrics, but in this case it is more obvious. Jersey and knitted fabrics usually have a nap to them; they also have a lot of stretch and because of this need to be sewn with a modern machine that can be set to a stretch stitch — not for the beginner. Other fabrics to be avoided by reluctant sew-ers are pure silk (very expensive anyway); slippery feeling, fine Polyesters that really are difficult to handle; also loosely woven fabric — whether wool or cotton, it will be tricky to work with.

Once you have learnt to recognize the direction of a fabric, you will also realize that it seldom works well if you cut out a garment other than in the direction your pattern tells you. For example, gathers never hang right if your garment is cut so that the gathering is worked in the same direction as the selvedge — the gathers will always stick out; but it you gather across the fabric, your gathers are bound to hang well.

The safest fabric to start with is a firmly woven all-cotton fabric. It will handle easily when being cut out, pressed and made up and then will retain its crisp, fresh look when worn.

Lastly a word about interfacings (used to back fabrics in places where they need to be held firm and crisp or stiffening). Vilene is by far the most popular one. It comes in several weights, and there is even an iron-on one that saves you having the job of tacking your interfacing in place. Vilene is also very economical — there is no weave to it, therefore it doesn't matter which direction you cut out your required shape and you can use every last scrap of it.

The more old-fashioned types of interfacing are the crisp woven cottons such as Victoria lawn. Because this type of interfacing has to be cut with the direction of the fabric in mind and generally speaking has to be treated almost as carefully as the fabric of the garment itself, it does tend to be used by slightly more experienced dressmakers.

YOUR
SEWING
MACHINE

If you're not a dedicated needle-person, you probably won't want to spend several hundred pounds on a brand-new sewing machine. But I do recommend that you get hold of a second-hand one. They were very well made in the old days, and even if you have to operate the machine by hand, it's much less hard work than sewing by hand. A lot of old Singer machines were later electrified, and they are a good buy; another good old-fashioned machine is Frister & Rossman. These old machines won't do anything fancy, like buttonholes, but they'll sew the long seams of curtains, for instance, beautifully.

Even if your machine is quite elderly, it is well worth looking after. A little know-how and attention to detail will keep it running smoothly and it will give good service for all your basic sewing needs. Oil the machine regularly (our diagram gives the main oiling points, but check in the instruction booklet that your machine is the same). Remove top and bobbin threads before doing so. The oiling points are clearly marked in red on most machines and a few drops of oil in each is all that is required. (Do make sure you use sewing machine oil!) After oiling, run the machine fast for a few minutes to ensure that the oil has penetrated and any surplus will have run through. Never use **too much** oil, it will just continue to run through the machine and mark your sewing. Little and often is the motto here. If the machine has been stored in the cold, before using it, bring it into a warm room and put the machine light on for a short time.

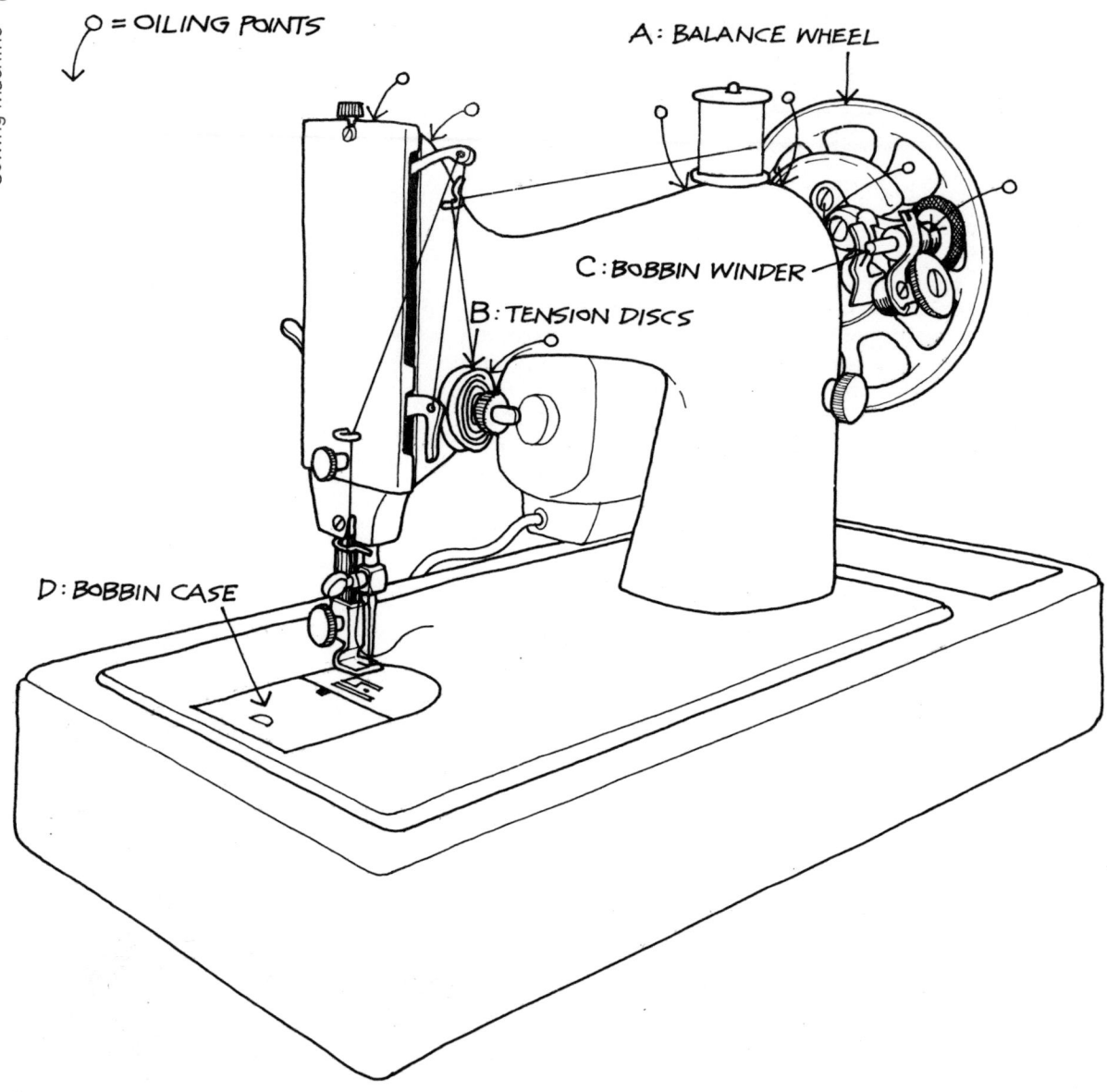

○ = OILING POINTS

A: BALANCE WHEEL

C: BOBBIN WINDER

B: TENSION DISCS

D: BOBBIN CASE

Threading the Machine
Before threading the machine, turn the balance wheel (A) by hand so that the needle is at its highest point, then make sure that the thread runs between the tension discs (B) and not to one side of them. Thread the needle from left to right.

Don't forget to wind the bobbin with the same thread. Use the bobbin winder (C), which is usually set to the front of the balance wheel. Then place the bobbin in its case (D). The thread is then taken back through the slot and under the tension spring. Then, holding the upper thread loosely in your left hand, turn the balance wheel once with your right hand in order to bring the bobbin thread up ready to sew.

A : BALANCE WHEEL

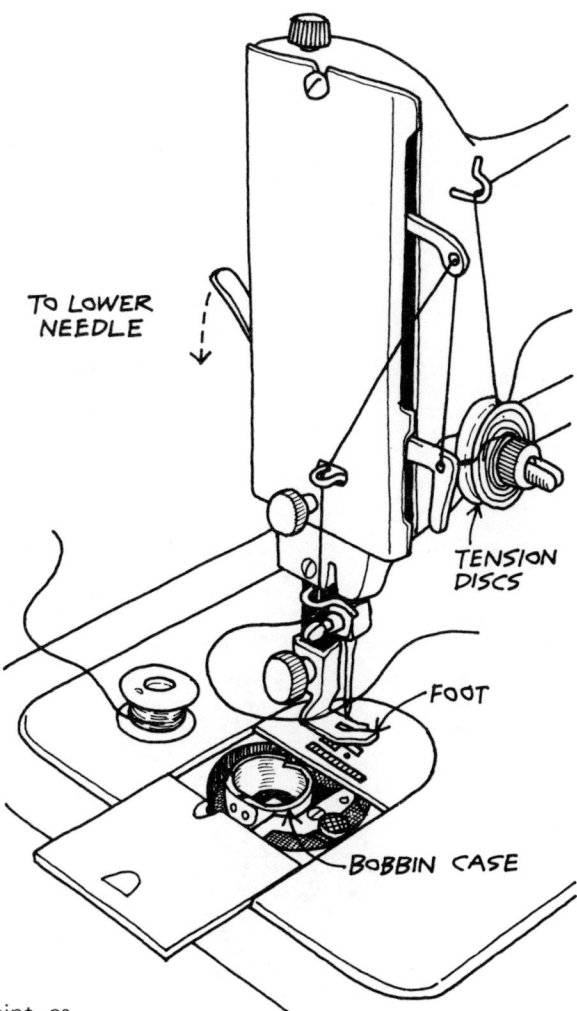

TO LOWER NEEDLE

TENSION DISCS

FOOT

BOBBIN CASE

Sewing

Before starting to sew, with the needle at its highest point, as explained, take both the upper and bobbin threads to the back of the foot away from you. With foot raised, insert fabric with the bulk of it to the left so that you don't have to feed it through the limited space to the right of the foot. Lower the foot and stitch away. To pivot the work (to change direction), whilst sewing, make sure the needle is down into the work before raising the foot to turn the work.

Tension

One of the usual problems with an older sewing machine is getting the tension right. If it's not right, then you might as well sew by hand, because the imperfect stitches on the machine will show as weak, distorted sewing instead of being neat, even and straight — and they may easily come undone. It's easy to see if the tension is wrong, the line of stitches will be formed like this:

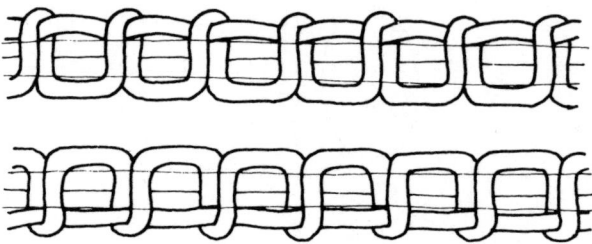

Both upper and lower tensions **must** be equal to give even stitching. Whether the tension is too tight or too loose, it can usually be adjusted by turning the small nut on the upper tension spring. Regulate the tension only when the pressure foot is down. Remember: lightweight fabrics require a light tension and heavier fabrics need more tension. The bobbin tension should rarely be altered.

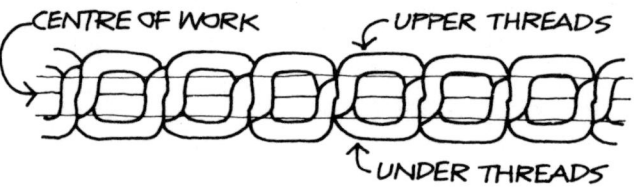

General

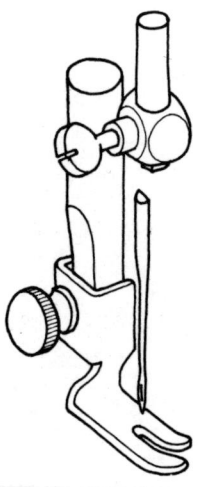

When replacing a needle, make sure that it is placed flat side first into the needle clamp. Before leaving your machine for any length of time, loosen the smaller wheel at the centre of balance wheel. In order to do this, hold the balance wheel as you turn the smaller wheel towards you.

BASIC STITCHES

HERRINGBONE STITCH

Starting Unless otherwise stated, work from right to left and always start by working a couple of small stiches one over the other in order to secure the working thread. For hems it is sometimes permissible to start with a small knot, though — especially when it is hidden by being taken through inside the turning.

Tacking Large stitches in contrast thread that hold the work in place before it is finally sewn.

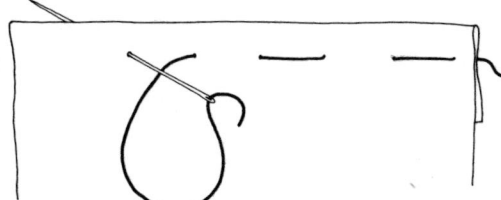

Hemming Used for holding a folded edge down in place.

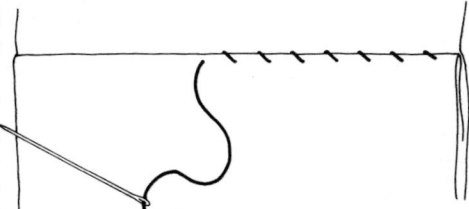

Running Stitch Used for straightforward seams, joining two edges.

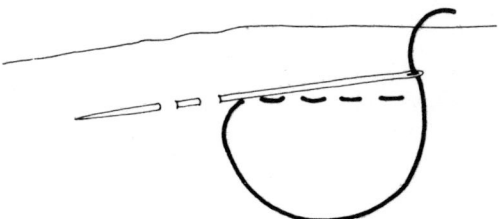

Back Stitch and **Half Back Stitch** Used for joining seams where greater strength is needed.

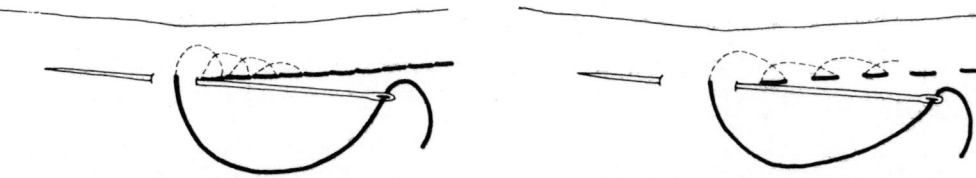

Overcasting The simplest way of neatening raw edges.

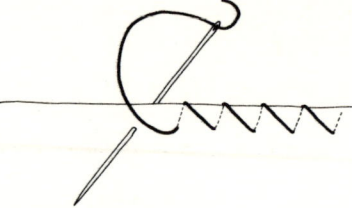

Buttonhole Stitch As its name implies, is for buttonholes and also for neatening raw edges.

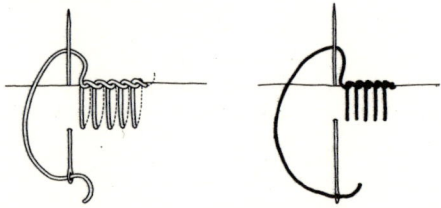

Slip Stitch Used for hems, picking up just one thread of the fabric above hem, the stitching is invisible on the right side.

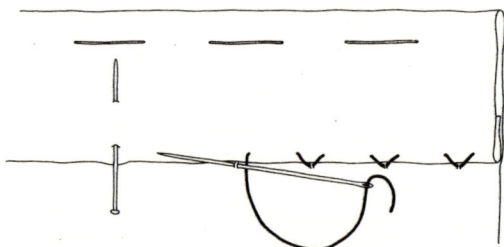

Catch Stitch Also used for hems, or loosely holding two edges together — as only one thread of the fabric is picked up from each side, then stitches are invisible on right side.

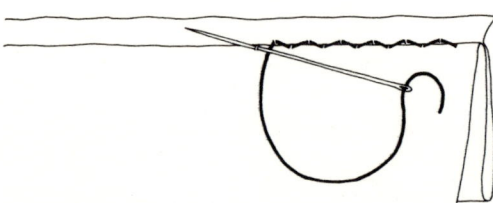

Herringboning Used for hems on heavier weight garments where extra strength is required; again only one thread of fabric is picked up so that the stitches are invisible on the right side. Work from left to right.

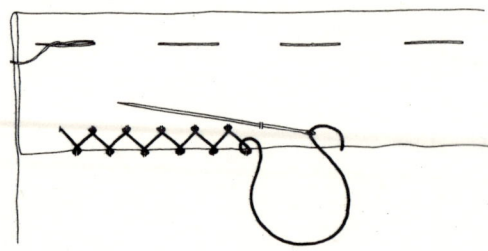

Finishing Finish as you started: by working two or three small stitches over each other to secure the thread before cutting it off on the wrong side.

MENDING AND PATCHING

ONCE YOU'VE STARTED DARNING THE WEFT IS EASY....

Depending on the type of tear and the kind of material, there are different ways in which a repair can be carried out neatly and maybe even invisibly. The important things to remember are: keep the stitches small and match your thread carefully.

Wools or Loosely Woven Fabrics

Use a very fine matching thread (ideally a few strands of the actual materials pulled from a seam allowance or the hem if either of these is ample enough). Follow the weave each side of the tear, drawing the edges together as you work and easing any short ends at the raw edges through to the wrong side of the work.

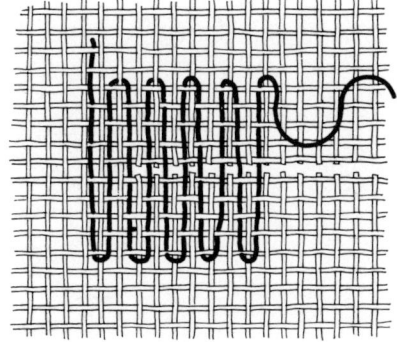

Cottons, Lawns or Fine Fabrics

Place a piece of very fine iron-on Vilene behind the tear with adhesive side to the wrong side of the tear — just sufficient to hold the edges together is all you need — and iron it in place. Now, using a suitable thread in a blending colour for printed fabrics or a matching one for plain, zig-zag in short lines of stitches across the tear line. This can be done by hand or machine, but, if you are using a machine, be sure to stitch very slowly to control the length of the stitch lines and, with needle down, pivot carefully on an angle at the end of each line, thus controlling the spacing of the lines.

For either of the above methods, do remember that even if your tear is diagonal across the weave of the fabric, the stitches must follow the weave.

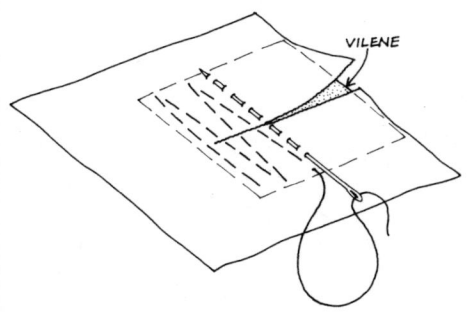

VILENE

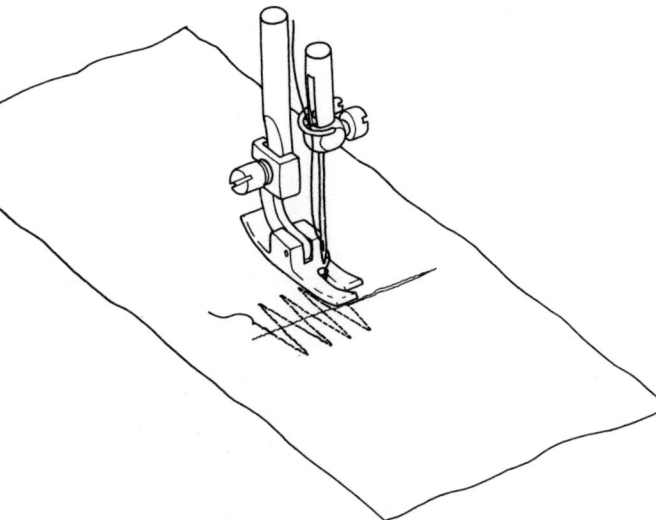

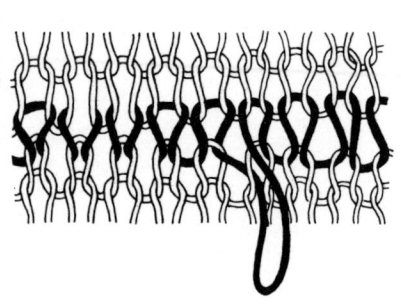

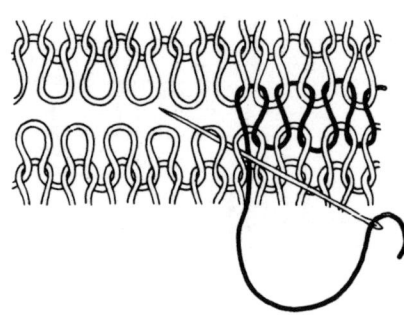

Knitted Fabrics

Sometimes with knitted fabrics the thread does not break, but is pulled up into an ugly loop, with a line of distorted stitches each side of it. Handled with care, this can be rectified. With a blunt-pointed sewing needle, or even a fine knitting needle, work first to one side of the loop, then the other and gradually loosen first one stitch using some of the loop, then loosen the next stitch, still easing back the thread from the loop and so on until all stitches one side of the pulled loop are restored to their original size and you have used up half of the loop. Now work over the stitches the other side of the loop in the same way. The offending snag (which weakens the fabric) has now been removed and the fabric returned to its original look and strength.

For a fairly fine knitted fabric, use a tacking thread and loosely draw the torn edges together to hold them in place. Now, using a finer thread than that used in the knitted fabric, follow the 'weave' of the stitches each side as much as possible and tension the work stitch by stitch as you proceed. This way you will retain the elasticity of the fabric. Again make sure the edges meet neatly at the tear line and take any short, raw edges through to wrong side.

On a hand- or machine-knitted sweater it is sometimes just a thread that has been pulled horizontally across the fabric and then broken that causes the offending hole. In this case, if the fabric is not too fine, use a matching thread and graft the two sets of stitches together as in knitting.

If, after all, when placing the edges of any tear together, you find they do not meet (because of the untidiness of the tear), or if what you thought was a tear turns out to be a hole, then the answer is to patch it or disguise it . . .

Applying a Patch

There is really only one way to work a patch. First cut a piece of fabric slightly larger than the area to be patched. Turn under 5mm./¼ inch turnings all round the patch. Pin, then tack the patch over the hole on the right side of the fabric, matching the direction of the fabric. On the reverse side, again take 5 mm./¼ inch turnings around the hole, snipping corners if necessary and pin, then tack these edges to the patch. Hem around edges on both sides.

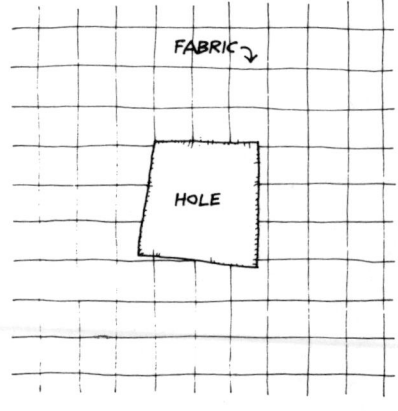

FABRIC

HOLE

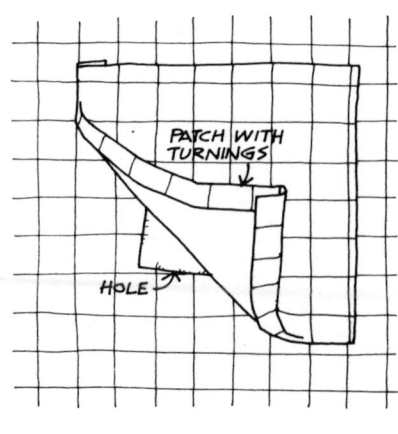

PATCH WITH TURNINGS

HOLE

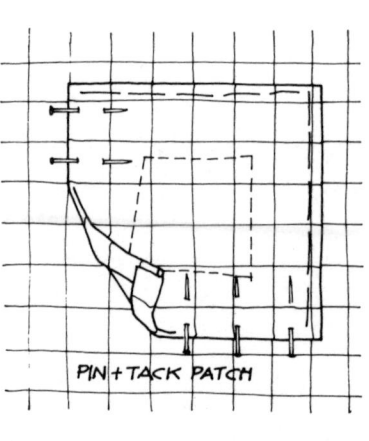

PIN + TACK PATCH

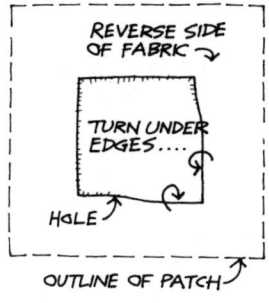

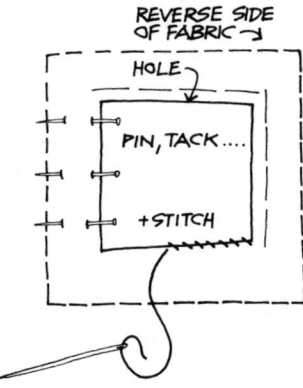

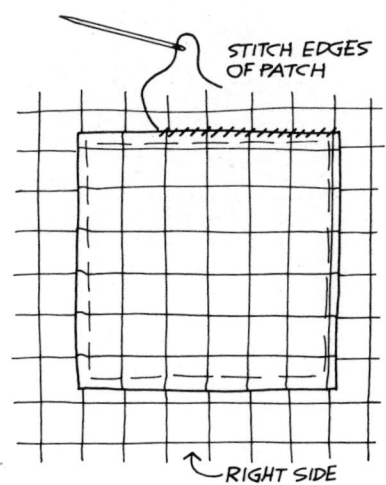

This basic patch, although durable and strong, can look very obvious. Since you can't hide it, why not make a virtue of it? On children's playclothes, and jeans, such a patch in a bright colour and sewn on to the right side of a garment can look fun. If, however, it is for example on a printed dress, there are one or two ways to make it look less conspicuous, although the actual method is very much the same. First of all, you must match the fabric. Look over the garment and see if there is a small piece of fabric that can be used. Perhaps there is a generous hem allowance on the dress and it can be made narrower, a shield behind a zip that can be removed and utilized, or even (more drastically) an inset pocket that can be taken out. Next, matching the pattern print as much as the size of your patching fabric will allow, cut your patch and place it on the *underside* of the garment; turn under the edges round the hole to the wrong side. This will avoid the hard, very straight line around the patch from standing out too much.

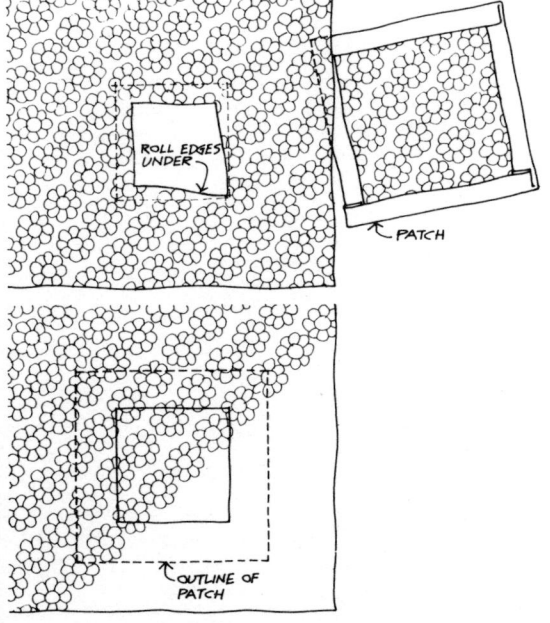

Heavy fabrics that are not too tightly woven can still be patched, but with a difference. Try fraying the edges of the patch, then darn the frayed strands through the fabric around the hole, then finish off the edges of the hole in the same way. Though this will thicken the area around the patch, it is far less bulky than a patch with turnings.

Now Disguising it All

Having mended your tear, or worked your patch, you might still find it looks rather obvious. So, if it is in a suitable place, why not cover it with a bold appliqué flower motif such as this? Or, if it is a rather plain garment, a plain pocket. Either could be in print fabric to go on plain or vice versa.

For a flower motif, first trace off the outline of the shape and cut it out in paper. Cut this shape in iron-on Vilene and iron it on to the wrong side of your material. Allowing 5 mm./¼ inch turnings all around the Vilene section, cut out. Turn under 5 mm./¼ inch (you will probably have to clip the curves down to the Vilene every so often for it to lie flat), place over patched area and first pin, then tack and finally hem in place. Press lightly and then stitch a few lines through the petals to keep it flat.

For a pocket, trace off the outline and cut it out in paper, marking in dotted line. Allowing 5 mm./¼ inch turnings, cut this shape in fabric, marking the dotted line with tacking through the paper and fabric. Cut through the tacking as you remove the paper. Turn under 5 mm./¼ inch all round, pin, then tack evenly. Fold the top of the pocket to the wrong side at marked line and slip stitch side edges. Press lightly. Place the pocket over the patch and pin, tack and hem in place. Finally, you can machine stitch the pocket, but take care to keep the stitching even around the curve.

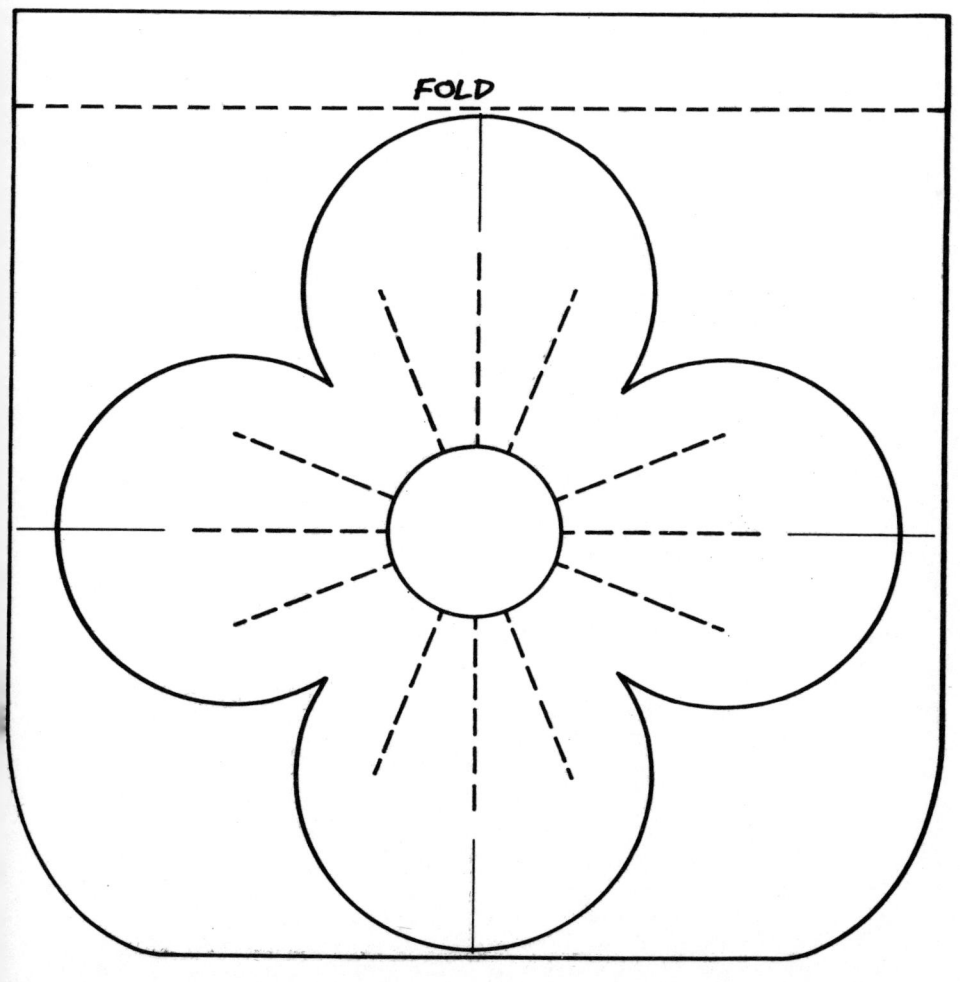

FOLD

FASTENINGS

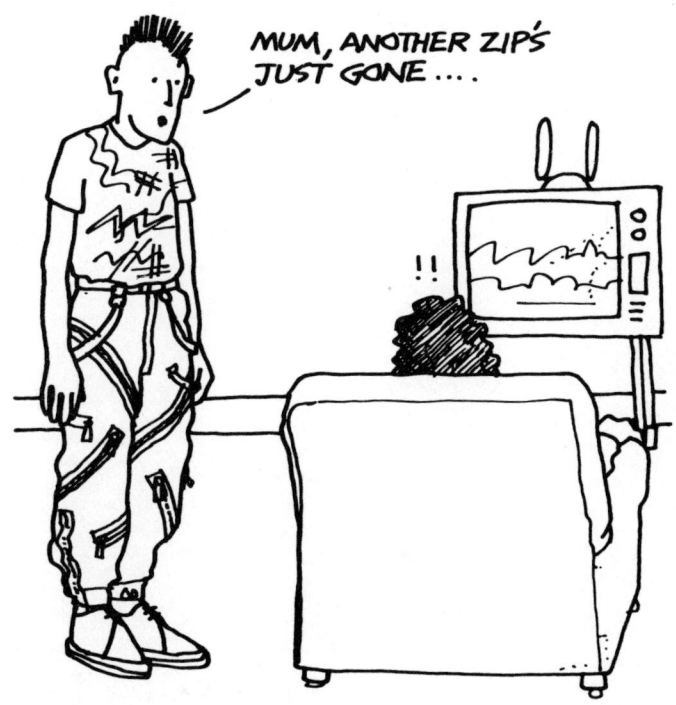

Each type of fastening has its own particular use and should be sewn on correctly, so don't be lured into 'making do'. The remarks here apply equally to replacing or putting on new ones. All fastenings come in a wide variety of sizes and metal ones are available in white (silvered) as well as black. Velcro (that wonderful 'touch and close' fastening you can use on heavier garments) is available in a wide choice of colours.

Hooks and Eyes

These are used to link edges that do not overlap. On wrong side of work, place the eye to the left-hand side with just enough of the loop extending over the edge to take the hook. Stitch each side of the ring just inside the edge to hold it in place, then sew down the rings with buttonhole stitches. The head of the hook half is placed to the edge of the right-hand side. Stitch over the neck of it just to hold it in place, then sew down the rings with buttonhole stitches in the same way as for the eye.

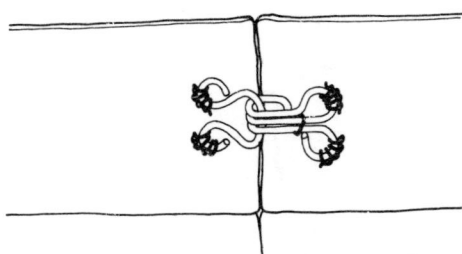

Hooks and Bars

These are used to fasten edges that do overlap. Sew the hook to the underside of the overlap in the same way as given above. Overlap the edges and mark the position for the bar on the underwrap, then sew the bar with buttonhole stitches.

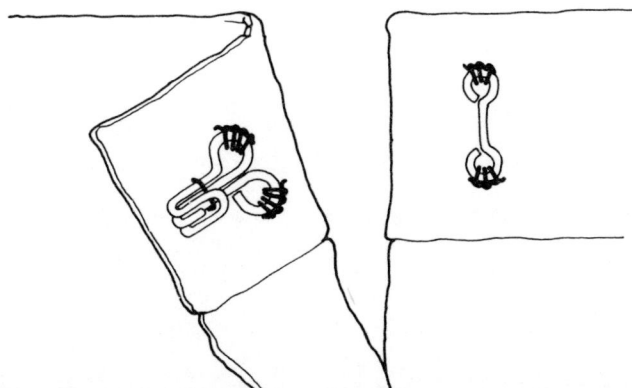

Press Fasteners

These are used on overlapping edges where there is little or no strain; they usually just neaten an overlapping edge.

Sew the thin side with the knob at the centre to the underside of the overlap with 3 or 4 small straight stitches. Overlap the edges to position the other side of the fastener, then sew this in place in the same way.

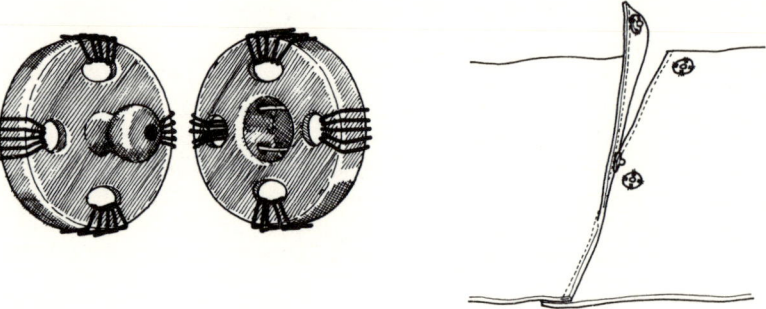

Velcro

This is a nylon tape that parts into two strips. Both sides are burred so that they grip as they meet. It is mostly used for fastening the over-lapping edges of loosely fitting garments, for example, overalls and sportswear. It is much too clumsy to use on fine fabrics. Because of its resistance as it is pulled apart, it must be sewn on very firmly. Strongly and neatly stitch the burred (looped) piece to the underside of the overlap so that the stitches will not show on the right (upper) side. Next, if possible, machine stitch the matching (soft) piece sewn to the right side of the underwrap as this takes most of the strain.

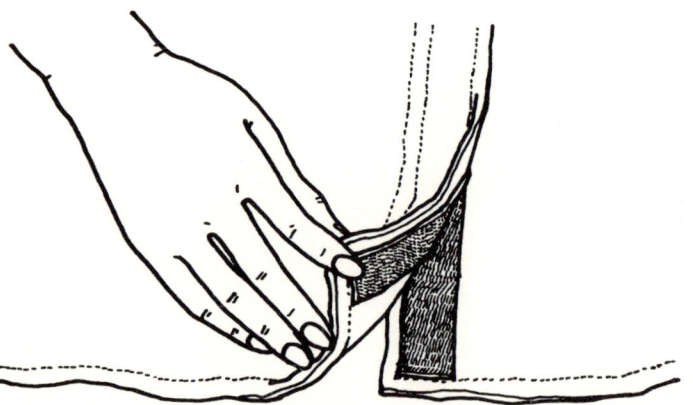

Buttons

Replacing Buttons
There is a huge variety of buttons available; so, before setting out to buy any, make sure you know exactly what you want. Do remember the diameter of a button should be approximately ⅔rds of the total length of the buttonhole it is to be fastened through, certainly no larger. Though size is the major factor, the weight of a button is also important. A thin lightweight button, though it might be just the right size, can look very inadequate on a heavy velour or tweed coat. Similarly, small but heavy buttons will drag on the front of a finely woven blouse.

Buttons for Coats and Heavy Garments
When sewing these on, whether they are buttons with holes right through (pierced buttons) or whether the holes are at the back only (shank buttons), the thick material surrounding the buttonhole will need room to sit flatly under the button. Therefore the button must be attached to the coat loosely with quite a 'neck' of thread between the fabric and button. If you are doubtful whether you can keep your

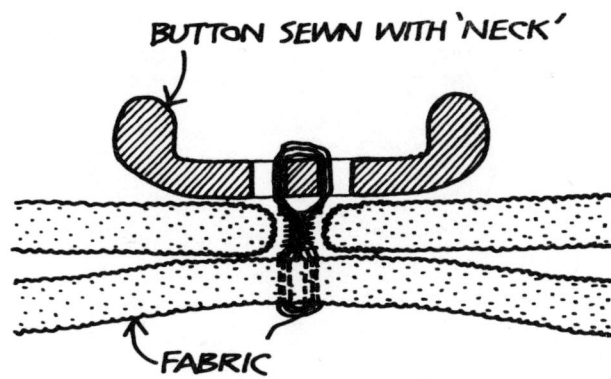

BUTTON SEWN WITH 'NECK'

FABRIC

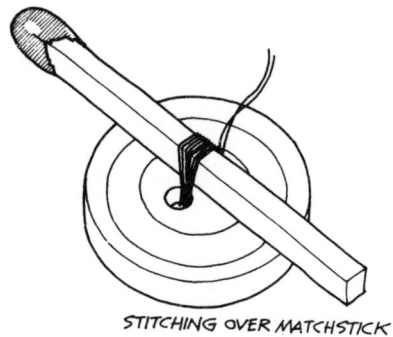

STITCHING OVER MATCHSTICK

stitches loose enough place a matchstick or orange stick over the top of the button and stitch over that. Before fastening off, you take the thread through to the underside of the button, remove the stick and wind the thread round and round the strands, forming the 'neck'. Finally take the thread through to wrong side of fabric and fasten off.

SHANK BUTTON

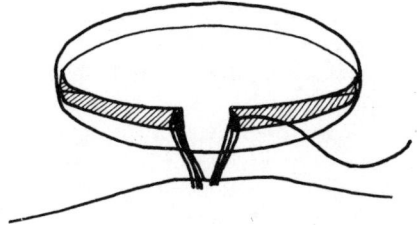

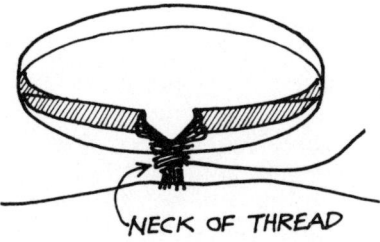

NECK OF THREAD

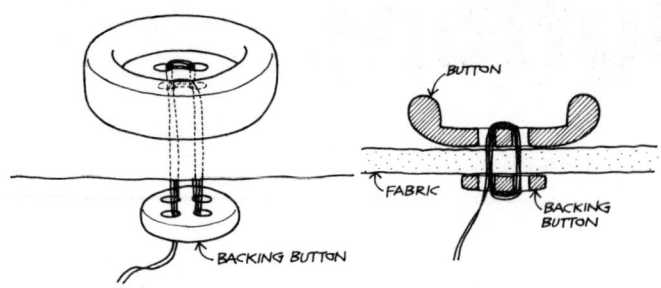

Sometimes, if a button is to be sewn to a loosely woven fabric, or even a single thickness of material, it will need a backing button. This is a small, clear, plastic button with the same number of holes (2 or 4) as the main button. It is sewn to the underside of the fabric *at the same time* as the button is sewn to the right side.

Dressweight Buttons

There is probably a wider variety of dressweight buttons than any other. Usually they are the correct weight for most knitteds too. If you are sewing buttons on to a loosely woven woollen or similar fabric, for added strength, take a small piece of fabric approximately 1 cm./½ inch by 2.5 cm./1 inch, fold it in half to form a square and place it on the wrong side of the fabric. Sew the button on through this doubled square of fabric.

Buttons for Shirts and Blouses

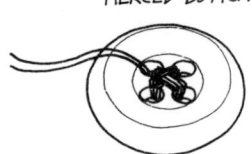

Shirt buttons are small 2- or 4-hole buttons with a slightly sunken centre. Mostly very plain, they are a good basic button to keep a supply of. For blouses, the choice is wider, but a good point to remember is that while plain fabrics can take plain or fancy buttons, printed fabrics really need just plain, toning buttons. Blouse buttons seldom need sewing on with a 'neck' as heavier garments do, but they should never be sewn on tightly. Always try to leave a little space between the button and fabric for the area around the buttonhole to sit flatly.

Covered Buttons

This is an ideal way to get perfectly matching buttons. The moulds now available make covering buttons child's play if you bear one or two things in mind. First of all, don't try to cover a button if the fabric is thick or stiff and therefore won't mould to the shape. Secondly do buy the moulds slightly smaller than the required button size — it is surprising just how much bulk is added by even the neatest covering. There is usually a diagram given on the back of the card the moulds are attached to which shows how big a circle of fabric to cut for your size of mould — be guided by this and you will avoid trying to push too much or stretch too little fabric over the teeth.

Zips

Replacing Zips
Hang on before you throw away that skirt, those trousers with the broken zip or take them to the nearest dressmaker to put in a new one — this really is a job you can do yourself.

First, make sure that you replace your broken zip with one that is both the right length for the opening and the correct weight for the garment. If the zip is too short, it will strain at the base and eventually break. If it is too light in weight, the strain on it will be too much and the same applies — it will break. On the other hand, if the zip is too heavy, although it may last well, it will look clumsy and drag the surrounding fabric. There is quite a choice of zips to be had. Fine ones are usually made of nylon and the medium and heavyweight ones are metal. You should be able to get a matching colour.

How to Set About it
For most garments (except trousers, which are explained below), there are two popular ways to insert a zip and they are given here. No matter which method you use, you must first remove the old zip and then press back the seam allowance surrounding the opening. Pin, then tack the zip in place to make sure it is set straight and even. Always stitch on the right side of the garment from the top of the opening down and fasten off all ends at each stage.

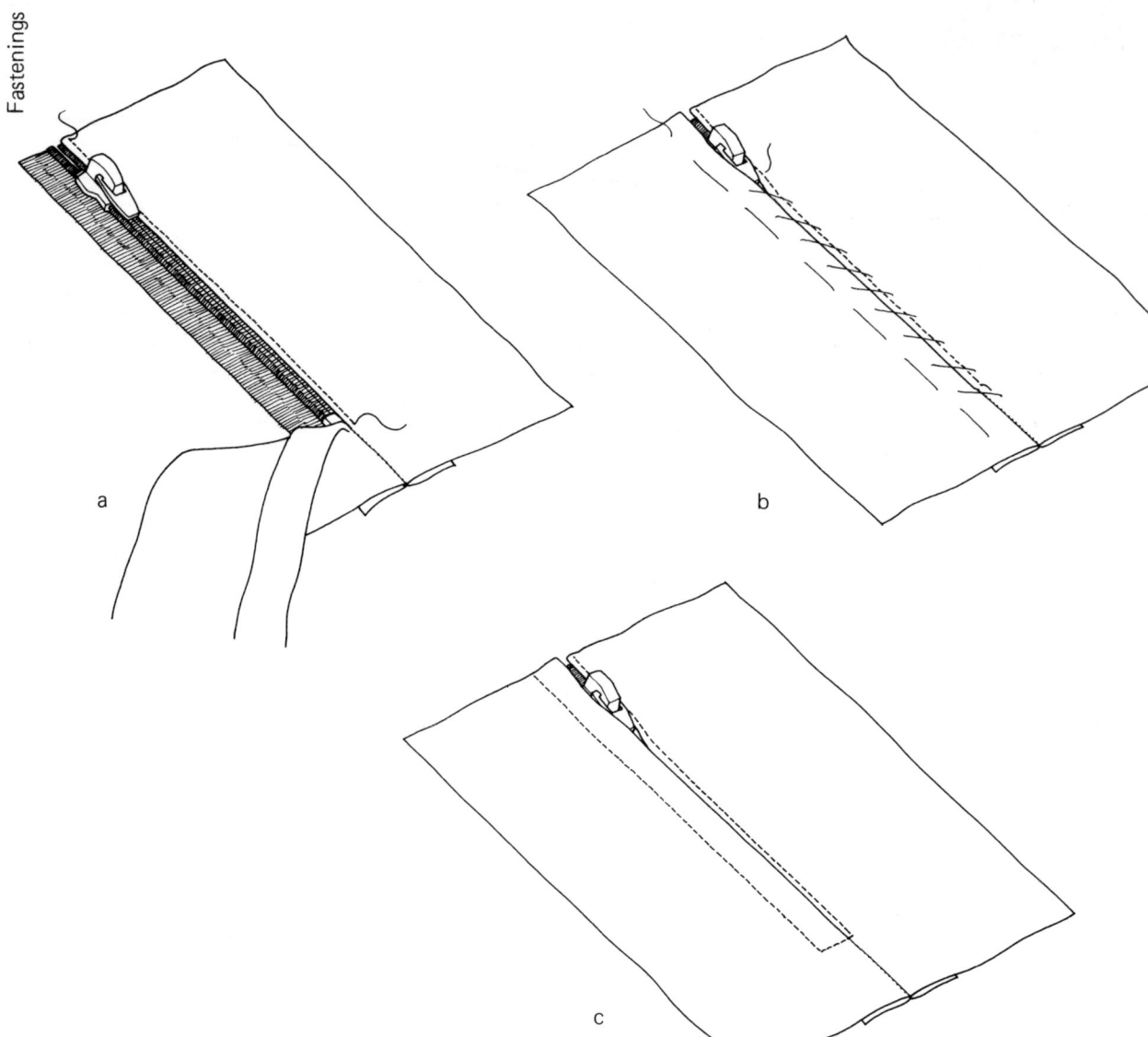

a

b

c

This way is usually used for side and centre back fastenings to both skirts and dresses. First pin, then tack the zip in place down right-hand side close to the fold of fabric and teeth of zip. Stitch about 3mm./⅛ inch from folded edge. Next, lap the left-hand edge over the zip teeth. Pin, then tack 1 cm./½ inch from folded edge, then, just to hold everything in place, loosely tack the two folded edges together with larger over-sewing stiches. Stitch down the left-hand side, but, as you reach the lowest point, with needle down into the work, raise the foot and pivot the work and stitch across the base to lowest point of stitching on right-hand side.

Slot Method

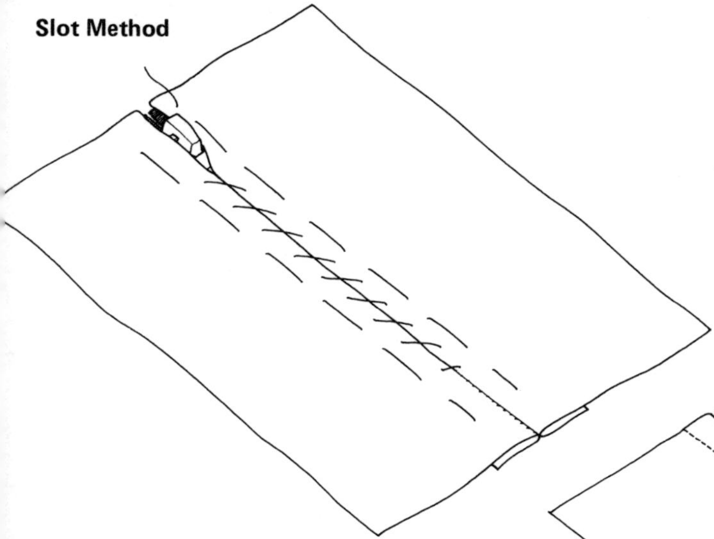

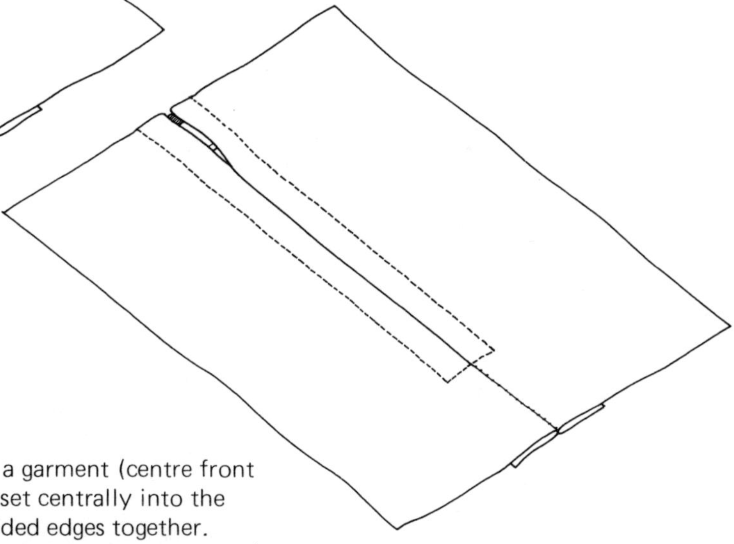

Generally used when a zip is placed centrally on a garment (centre front or back), or for cushion covers, etc, as the zip is set centrally into the opening. First of all, loosely oversew the two folded edges together. Place the zip centrally behind this, pin, then tack the zip in place 1 cm./ ½ inch from folded edges down both sides. Stitch the right-hand side first down to the lowest point; with needle down into the work, raise the foot, pivot then stitch to centre seam. Finish the left-hand side to match, making sure the stitching meets at the centre. Finally, if required, stitch across the top of the zip.

Sometimes for very sheer or fine fabrics, it is best to sew the zip in by hand. Use a half back stitch for extra strength and follow either of these methods.

Trouser Zips

Replacing a trouser zip can be a very tricky business and it must be machined for strength. When trousers are made, the very first step is to join the base of the centre front seam and insert the zip and all the seams are joined afterwards. You will therefore appreciate that as you work various lengths of seams will have to be unpicked as you insert your zip. First you must unpick the stitches of the waistband as you remove the broken zip. The new zip can then be pinned and tacked into place between the shield (the piece of fabric at the back) and the right-hand side of the opening, but in order to do this you will probably find you need to undo some stitching at the base of the zip. Machine stitch the zip in place on this side, 3 mm./⅛ inch from folded edge.

Now pin back the shield attached to the right-hand side to prevent it being caught in the stitching and pin, then tack and machine stitch the left-hand side, following the original sewing line. Lastly, replace all stitching and secure all layers in position with a few strong stitches across the base.

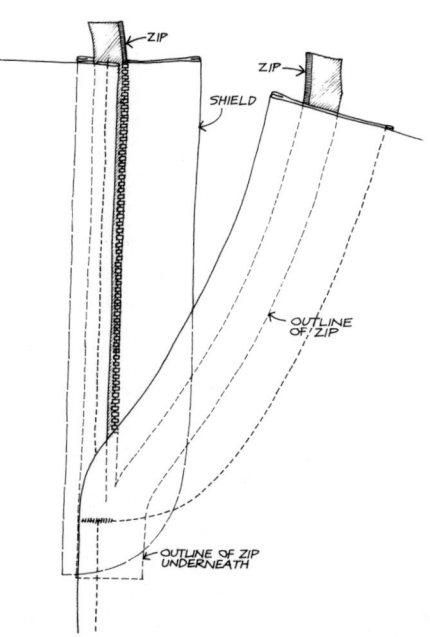

REPAIRS TO
LEATHER, SUEDE OR SYNTHETIC SKIN

Working with leather is much easier than you might think. But you *must* use the correct materials and observe one or two simple rules when actually sewing.

Equipment

First of all, you must use a leather needle. Available for both hand and machine sewing, they come in a choice of sizes from fine ones for sewing such things as gloves, to medium ones for sewing clothing, to really coarse ones for handbag repairs, etc. They have a three-sided point and this pierces the leather easily and the leather does not split (a common danger). Do try to match the thread already used as stitches on leather invariably show, but if the choice is left to you, use pure silk for hand sewing and draw the length of thread you are going to use through a block of beeswax (obtainable from haberdashers). This strengthens the thread and helps to avoid slip-knots and tangles as you sew. For machine sewing, use Coats button thread: a mixture of Polyester and cotton, it is a smooth yet strong thread. Finally, even if up to now you have got by without using a thimble, unless you want perforated fingers, you'll find you need one now.

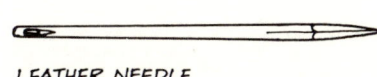

LEATHER NEEDLE

Sewing Methods

For most sewing on fairly soft leathers such as jackets, gloves, etc., use a stab stitch. This involves taking the needle through the work one stage at a time — it's time consuming, but necessary — in this way: start with a small knot at the end of your thread and place this between the two layers of skin. Stab the needle straight through the front layer only and draw the thread through, then, with threaded needle in front of work,

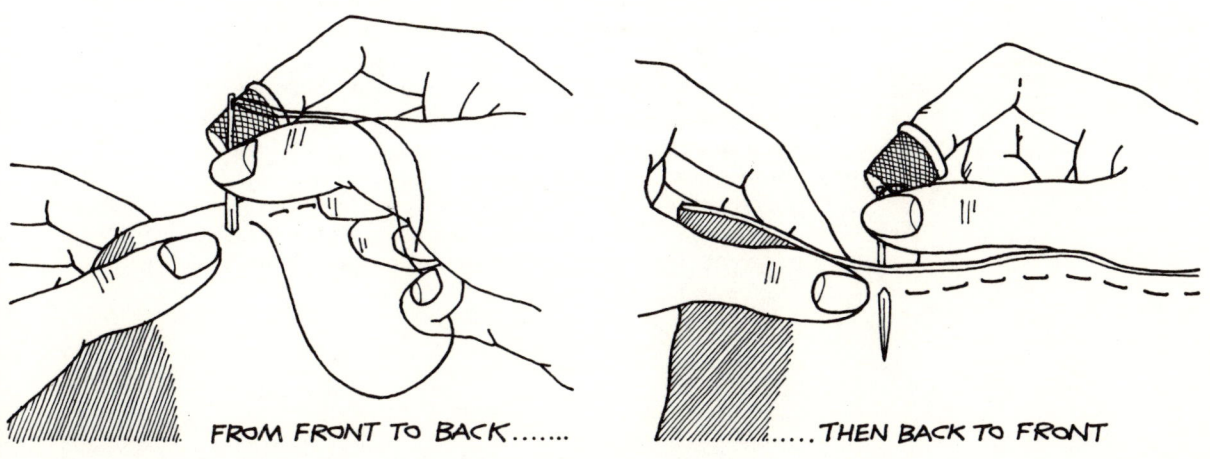

FROM FRONT TO BACK.......   .....THEN BACK TO FRONT

stab the needle straight through the work to the back and draw the whole length of the thread through to the back (not too tightly), then move along and make your next stitch from the back of the work straight through to the front. **Never** attempt a running stitch, the sewing will look very uneven and, as the leather will be pierced at an angle, the stitches will not be very strong. It is most important as you sew to pierce the skin straight through from one side to the other and **never** at an angle. Finish by working a couple of buttonhole stitches round the last stitch worked on wrong side of garment. A half back stitch can also be recommended for sewing leather, where only the top side of the work will show, but again it must be worked in the series of separate actions of stab stitching. When repairing gloves, use only the finest needle and thread and keep the stitches as small as possible, though as glove leathers are very soft and fine, you will have to be careful not to split the leather by making your stitches too small. If you have to replace a button, it is a good idea to check that all of them have a backing button (see page 38). These give added strength and will help prevent the leather splitting if the button is pulled.

Handbag repairs can very often be carried out at home, especially if it is a case of the stitching having come undone, when you can re-use the existing holes, which makes life easier. In this case, undo a few more stitches each side of the section to be repaired and, if possible, take the ends through to the wrong side between the layers of leather. Now with the needle and new thread (remember the beeswax) to the front, take the needle straight through the first stitching hole to back. With a separate length of waxed thread lying across the back of the work, loop the needle and thread around this and back through the same hole again to front. Move along to next hole and repeat the process. Finally, take these ends through to wrong side between layers and finish off all ends strongly.

There are other small bag repairs that can be carried out at home. Most handicraft shops sell D rings for repairing handles and rivets for fixing the handles. These rivets are sold with a small attachment that enables you to hammer them in place.

WAXED THREAD ACROSS BACK OF WORK ....

......WITH NEW THREAD LOOPED AROUND

Leather patches

Leather patches for elbows and binding for cuffs are splendid for renovating a jacket or sweater that has hard wear. Although these can be bought and very often have the sewing directions with them, you can, with an oddment of leather, make your own. To make the patches, cut two rectangles of leather 13 cm./5 inches by 10 cm./4 inches. Round the corners off slightly. (To do this trim a corner of one rectangle, fold it in half and use this corner to trim next one, and so on. Use this whole rectangle as a pattern for the second one.) Pin on the patch, using as few pins as possible, as they do mark the leather, and stab stitch a line following the edge of the patch. Cuff bindings need to be at least 2.5 cm./1 inch wide but the strips can be cut quite economically from an oddment of leather, as there is no grain direction to worry about as there is with fabric. Place the binding over the cuff as shown. Again using as few pins as possible, pin, then stab stitch through leather, fabric and leather in one action.

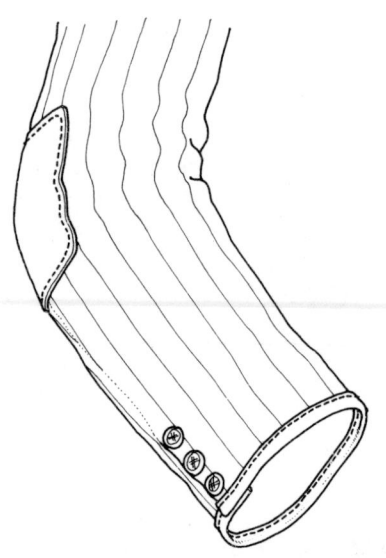

ALTERATIONS

Although alterations sound a bit like the age of austerity, you probably find yourself faced with them more often than you'd like. Fashion is mostly to blame. Trousers have changed so fast that a favourite pair of what were straight trousers had to be bell-bottomed and finally tapered. Skirt lengths shoot up and down and few can afford to buy new skirts every time the ankle length turns into the knee length and then to the mini skirt. There are other alterations that are explained by the unfortunate cause of change of shape. You may even have made a mistake in the shop and bought something that didn't really fit you, though you persuaded yourself that it did. Then, nowadays, we are all faced with taking up hems. Manufacturers seem to have given up attempting to hem jeans and casual trousers. You'll have to master a few elementary skills.

Obviously, the more drastic an alteration is, the harder it is to carry out successfully, so bear in mind that it's better to add or take in a little and succeed than to be too ambitious and spoil the garment altogether.

There is another important point to take into consideration: if your garment has been made of a fabric that has a synthetic content, or in fact if it is wholly synthetic, then it will have acquired a permanent 'crease' at any fold when first the garment was pressed during manufacture. This cannot be removed, and it may be very hard to disguise, so bear it in mind before you start. It means you will have difficulty in letting out or down.

When trying on a dress or skirt in order to lengthen or shorten it — or even just to straighten it — then do stand very erect in order to obtain a true line. Allow 'movement' room and don't take it in too tight. Also remember that stitching might take in a seam more than a line of pins.

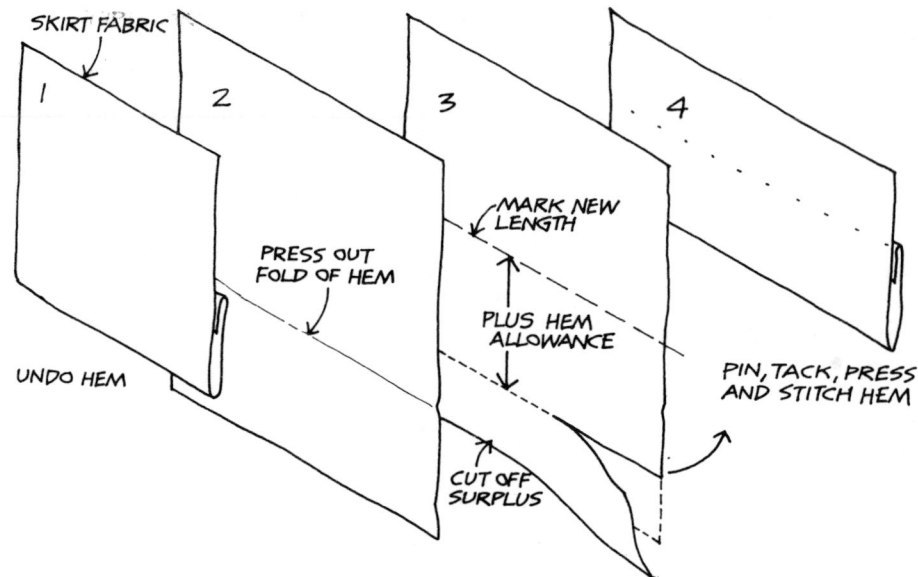

Although it might appear to be a case of simply undoing the hem and then taking it up again with a deeper hem allowance, this can sometimes look very heavy and clumsy. Try, if possible, to keep to the same depth of hem. Make a note of what measurement this is before you start. Undo the hem and press out the fold-of-hem crease. Try the dress or skirt on and have someone mark around the skirt (with tailor's chalk or pins) to the correct length. Next, add to this new line the hem allowance that you had originally and again mark all round. Cut away the surplus fabric below this. Pin up the hem, tack and press. Slip stitch or herringbone stitch the hem in place.

Lengthening a Skirt
First, the simplest way of all. Just let the hem down, press out the fold-of-hem crease, pin as before and turn up a narrower hem.

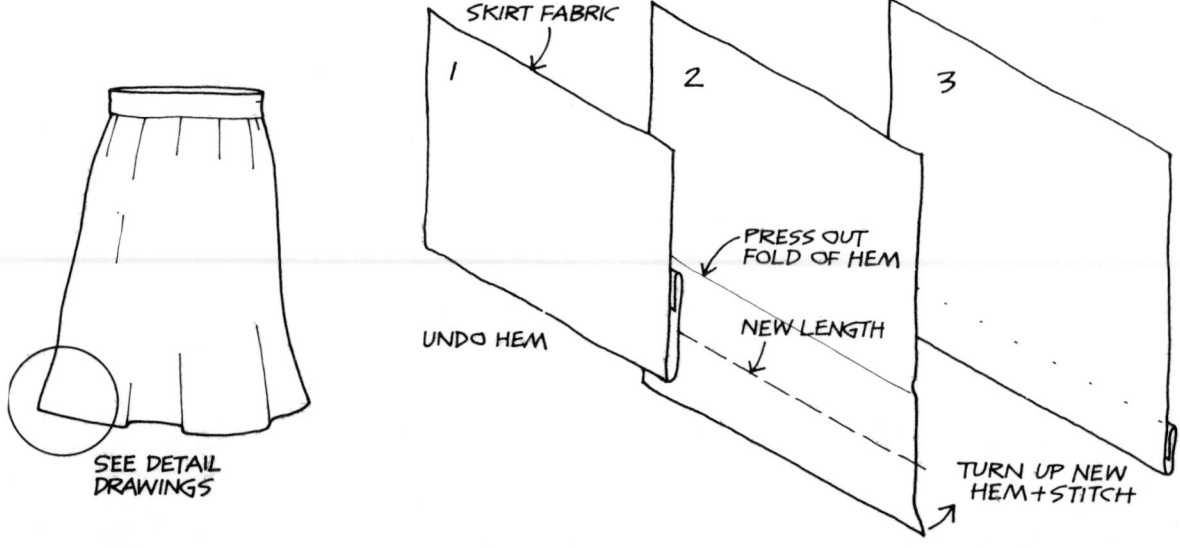

If you haven't enough material, you could add a false hem. For this, the false hem should be of a slightly finer fabric bias cut, that is to say, cut diagonally across the weave. This gives it more stretch and makes it mould more readily to the line of a hem. It is a method most recommended for skirts that are bias-cut to begin with, or for very full skirts. The bias strips for the hems should be at least 2.5 cm./1 inch wider than the depth you want the hem to be. This will allow sufficient for the turning each side. You will need to join lengths of bias hem together in order to obtain the total length you require. When doing this, make sure the ends follow the weave of the fabric and are cut diagonally. Place these ends at right angles to each other and join them along this diagonal line. Now, having unpicked your hem and pressed out the fold line, simply join right side of hem to right side of garment and sew one edge of the bias hem around the lower edge. Next, roll under the new seam at lower edge (to hide it), pin and tack in place. To complete the hem, turn under the remaining edge, pin, tack and slip stitch or herringbone stitch down.

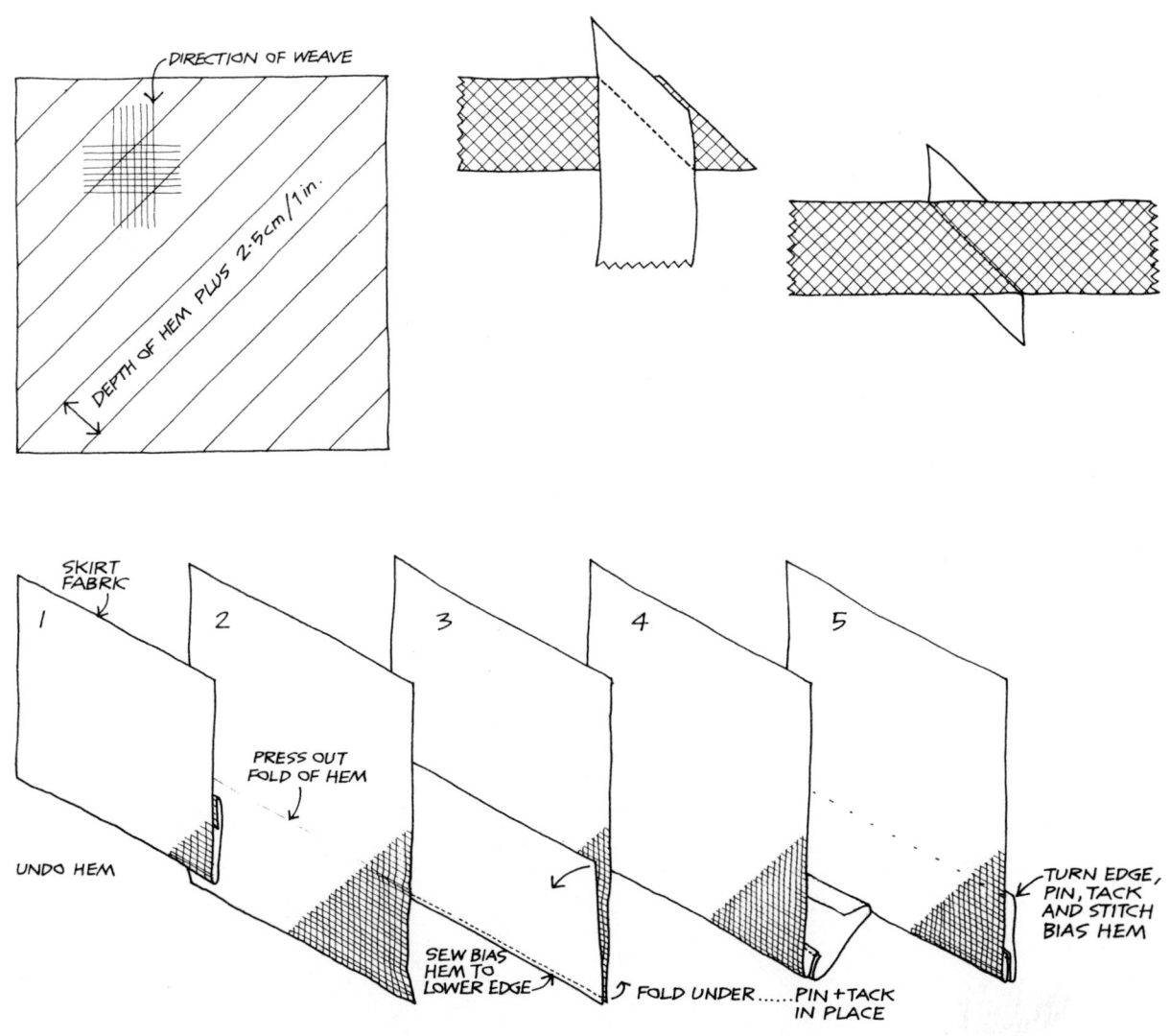

DIRECTION OF WEAVE

DEPTH OF HEM PLUS 2·5 cm / 1 in.

SKIRT FABRIC

1   2   3   4   5

PRESS OUT FOLD OF HEM

UNDO HEM

SEW BIAS HEM TO LOWER EDGE

FOLD UNDER...... PIN + TACK IN PLACE

TURN EDGE, PIN, TACK AND STITCH BIAS HEM

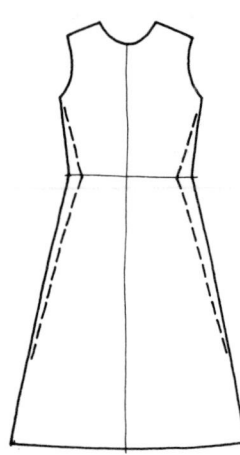

Making a Waist Smaller

The important thing to remember here is to make sure that the alteration is evenly balanced on both sides, or you'll end up looking lopsided, and your dress won't hang straight. First try the dress on and have someone pin in the amount to be removed at the waist. However, it's not just a question of taking the waist in, unless the skirt is a gathered one. If you just take the waist in, then it will bulge out in an ugly way above and below. So you must taper the line of pins above (if a dress) and below. And do remember the room you must leave yourself to move and so don't make it too tight. Still working on the right side of the garment, mark the pinned line with a line of tacking. Turn to wrong side. Clip through, but do not remove tackings, then unpick the side seams to just within the ends of the marked lines. Rejoin the seams on lines of tacking threads. To carry out this kind of alternation might entail the removing and replacing of a zip (see page 39) or waistband (see below).

Making a Waistband Smaller

If only a small amount needs taking out, it is possible first to remove the waistband and then replace it, having re-sewn the seam or adjusted the fastenings so as to reduce it, in the same way as it was originally sewn on, in doing so, ease in a slight fullness of the skirt/trousers all around, thus making the waistband smaller, leaving the same width in the skirt/trousers itself. If a more drastic alteration is required, again remove the waistband, then remove some of the fullness of the skirt/ trousers in the same way as 'Making a Waist Smaller', then finally replace the waistband.

Making a Waist Larger

If only a small amount is needed, the least drastic way is simply to undo the seam at both sides for about 25 cm./10 inches (or down to the hipline) and, starting at the original stitching line on the hips, pin, then tack and line up to the waist, tapering this outwards so that there is less in the seam and more in the waist. The side seams can then be rejoined on this new line. Of course in order to do this, you might need to remove and replace a side zip (see page 39) and you will have to find a little more to put in the waistband (see below).

Making a Waistband Larger

This is more difficult to do as you need to find the extra fabric to add to the waistband. However, as you remove the waistband, remove also the shield of fabric that lies behind the zip (most bought skirts have one). This precious piece of fabric can be utilized to add to the waistband and all you will need is a small piece of waistband stiffening to add to that already in the waistband.

If you need to add to the skirt itself, having removed the waist-band, let out the seams as for 'Making a Waist Larger'. To replace the waistband, completely undo one end of it, add the waistband stiffening and the extra fabric and replace.

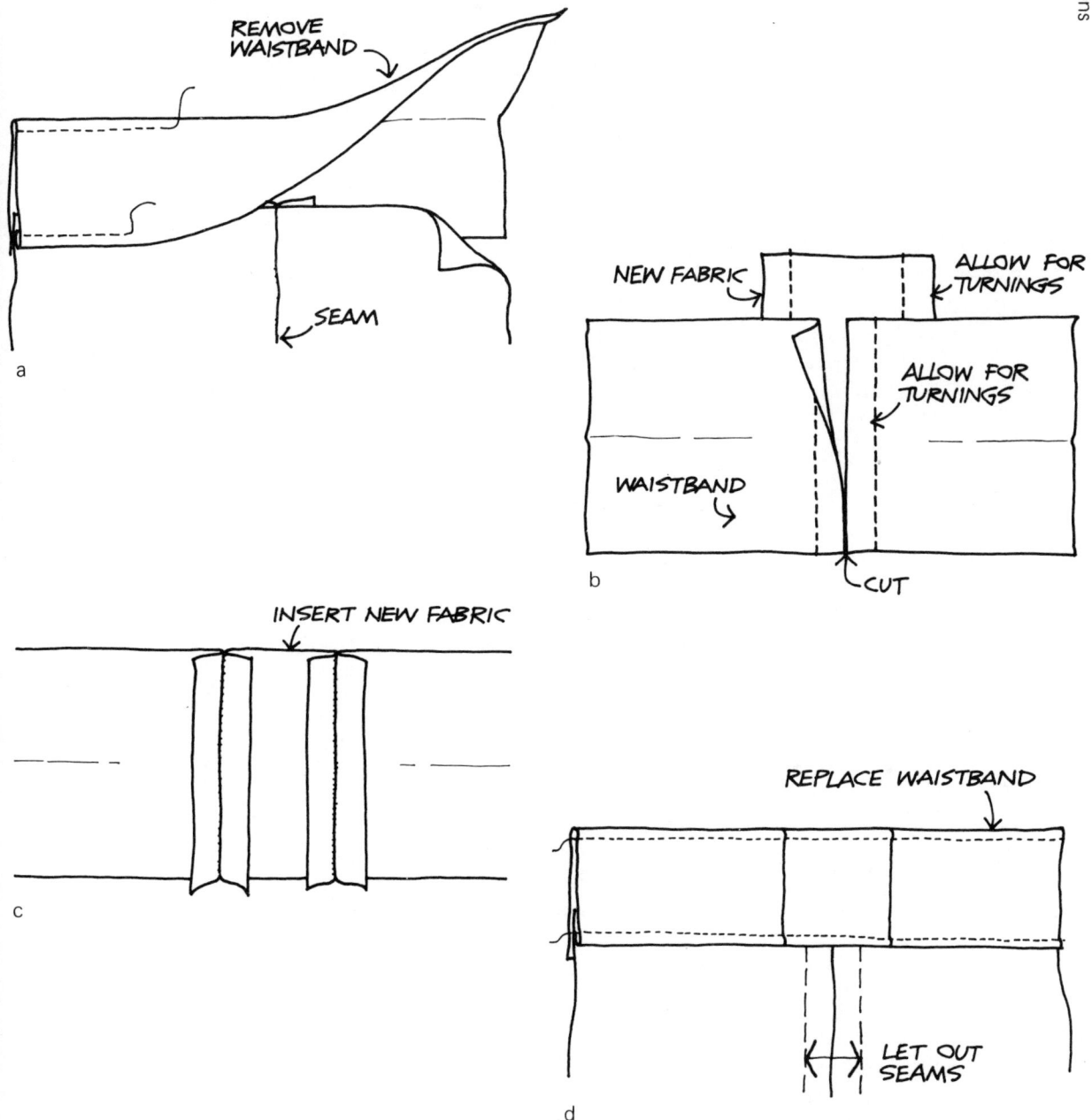

a

b

c

d

CURTAINS

Heavy curtains can add tremendously to the furnishing of a room. They don't even have to be made of very expensive fabric, but if it suits the room and they are well made so that they hang well, they will look expensive.

Before Buying Your Curtaining

One or two things to watch out for. If you choose a print material be sure to buy sufficient not only to match the pattern on the widths that are to be joined together, but also at the sides of the curtains that butt up together, so that the pattern will match as they hang together. This might seem an expensive business, buying fabric in excess of what you actually need, but the short lengths you discard (no matter how short) can be made, with the help of a little toning plain fabric, into matching cushion covers (see page 70).

     If you are fixing new curtain track, try to have sufficient track extending beyond the window to enable the curtains to be full enough to hang, when drawn back, half over this area and half over the window.

Lengths Required

First of all the drop. That is the length from curtain track to either the floor (if you want full-length curtains) or the windowsill. Measure this length and add on to it 2.5 cm./1 inch to turn over at the top for the tape and 10 cm./4 inches at the lower edge for the hem. This total length is for one width of material. Now for the total width. For a gathered heading (the most usual sort) you will need at least 1½ times the width of the window area to be covered, i.e. the length of the curtain track. As you are governed by the width the curtaining comes in, err on the generous side, having more in the width rather than having less. If you are making your curtains in pairs, have the same width in both, even if this means cutting one width in half along its length and adding one of these to each curtain to even them up. The total amount to buy then, is the number of widths multiplied by the length. Remember the extra you will need if matching a pattern.

Preparing to Make Them

To give a smooth unbroken line to the curtains as they hang, all sewing on the selvedges (or edges) and hem *must* be done by hand and preferably slip stitched. If the selvedges appear to pucker slightly, just snip them through every so often to make them lie flat. The only machine stitching should be the rows across the top sewing on the curtain tape (only for strength) and the seams that join the lengths of material. Velvets and velours must always be made with the pile or nap lying upwards. This adds depth and richness to the colour as the light shines on it. As a general rule, it is a good idea to make up any plain curtaining so that it lies in one direction. Sometimes a slight nap or way of fabric is not very apparent at first, but when made up into a wide expanse of curtaining it can become very obvious. And do check that the pattern (if there is one) will hang correctly before you sew on your tape. It's annoying to find the flowers on your curtains growing downwards when you hang them up.

Simple Unlined Curtains

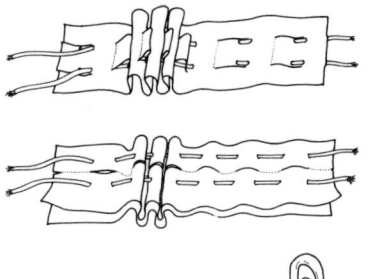

First cut off your lengths and join them, right sides together, by machine, into the widths required. Next, turn under the selvedges along each side edge and slip stitch down. Turn under 2.5 cm./1 inch at the top of the curtain to the wrong side and lightly press. Allowing turnings, cut a length of tape to the width of the curtains. Pull out cord ends at one end of tape for about 4 cm./1½ inches and loosely knot them together without gathering the tape at all. Trim off half of the cordless end of tape to about 2 cm./¾ inch and turn this amount under. Place folded end to one end of curtain top and tack centrally over raw edge of curtain with about 1.5 cm./½ inch of folded curtain edge extending above. Finish other edge of tape to match, again loosely knotting the cord ends. Machine stitch along both sides of tape using a thread to match the curtaining. (A zipper foot is very useful for this.)

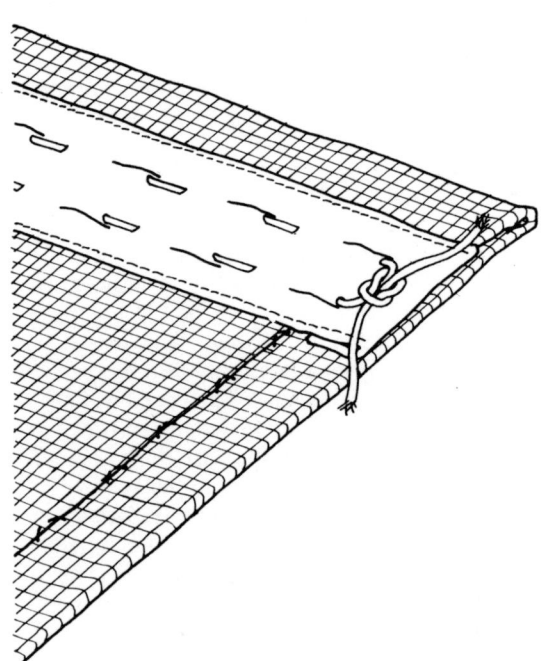

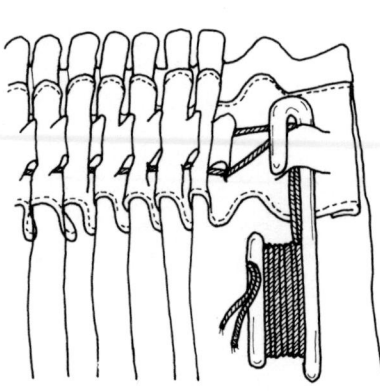

Lastly from one end undo the knotted cords and draw them up as required, and equalize the gathers but **do not** cut off the ends. You will need these to release, making the curtains flat for laundering or cleaning. There is a small gadget available which these cords will wind on to and can then be tucked out of sight. Hang the curtains and pin the hems to the length required; tack and then slip stitch hems as given previously (see above).

Lining Curtains

Curtain lining is an all-cotton, slightly glazed, rot-proof fabric. It usually is 120 cm./48 inches wide, and comes in two or three shades of beige which is suitable for most curtains and also in a limited range of colours. Buy the same length of lining as curtaining. Lined curtains always hang better than unlined, and provide a little more insulation. Also lining will prevent the curtains from fading, especially if the window is in a sunny position. As you cut off your lengths of lining, don't try to cut it by the weave as it is seldom straight. Simply cut straight across the fabric. There are several ways to line curtains and these are the methods most used:

Loose Lined

This way is the simplest and therefore the most popular. The lining hangs free from the curtain and is attached only by hooks through the special lining tape sewn on the top. This makes the linings very easy to remove for laundering. You will need lining tape to fit the width of the lining, in addition to the regular tape sewn to the curtain itself. Make the curtains as for unlined ones. Next, cut the lengths of lining the same length as the *finished* curtain. Having machine stitched the widths together, you can carry on and finish them by machine. First turn under the selvedges and machine stitch them. Leaving the hem till last, place the raw edge at top of lining between the two edges of the lining tape with the shorter side of the tape, with 2 rows of cord showing, uppermost and about 4 cm./1½ inches extending each end and machine stitch. Release the cords from ends; trim ends of cords to about 2 cm./ ¾ inch and turn under and slip stitch down on wrong side. Slip a few hooks through the tapes of both lining and curtain to obtain the length

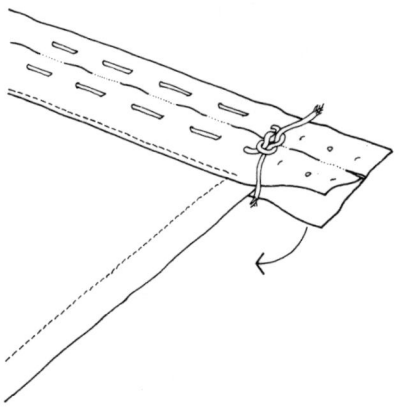

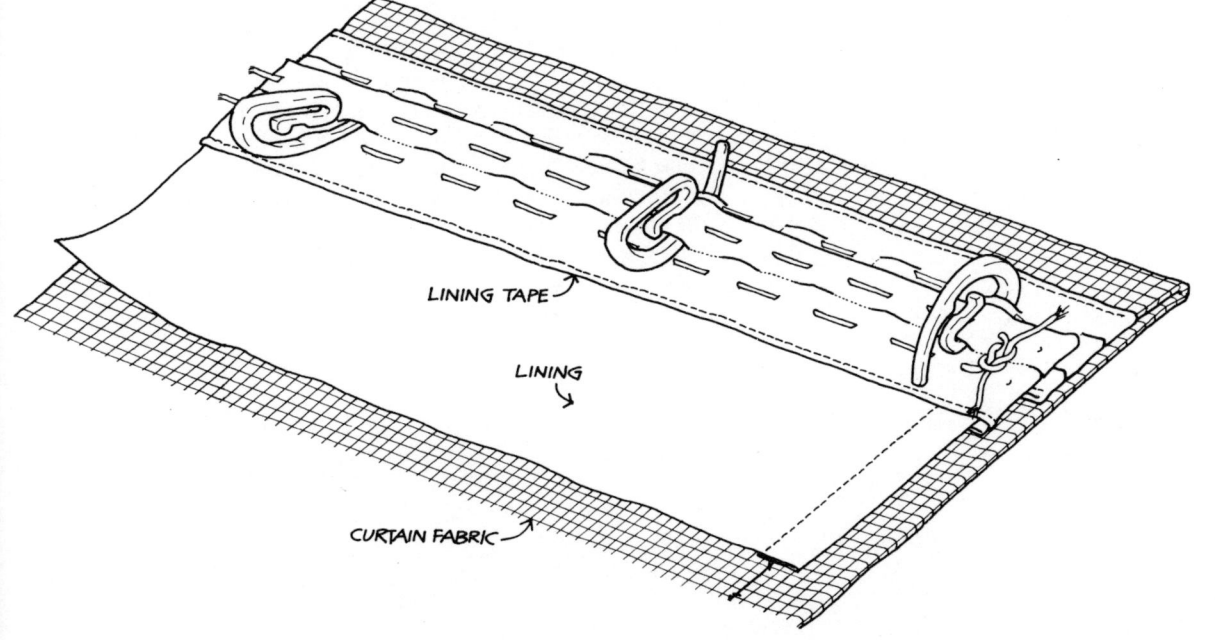

LINING TAPE

LINING

CURTAIN FABRIC

for lining. Turn up, pin, tack and slip stitch or machine stitch hem of lining making it about 5 cm./2 inches shorter than the curtain. Slip remainder of hooks in place. When drawing up the cords for both lining and curtain, pull the lining cords up very slightly tighter than for the curtain. Making the top of lining slightly narrower in this way will ensure none of it shows on the right side when the curtains are pulled to and fro.

Lining Attached

Cut off the curtain lengths and join them into widths required as before but do not finish the tops. Now, making them approximately 5 cm./2 inches shorter, cut and join the lining lengths in the same way. Turn under selvedges of both and press. Slip stitch down selvedges of curtains only. Now lay curtain flat with wrong side uppermost and turn over 2.5 cm./1 inch at top. Next, lay lining over curtain with right side uppermost and slip raw edge of lining under the 2.5 cm./1 inch of curtain top. With edges of lining just inside the folded side edge of curtain, sew on tape as given for unlined curtains, thus securing the lining. Turn up hem of curtain, pin, tack and then slip stitch in place. Making lining about 5 cm./2 inches shorter, turn up hem in the same way and machine stitch in place. Finally, pin, tack and slip stitch the folded lining selvedges down just inside the folded curtain edge.

Lock Stitched Linings

Truly reluctant needle-workers pass over this section, for a lot more work is entailed. The lining is attached to the curtain before it is made up by rows of *loosely* worked buttonhole stitches (lock stitching) in rows down the length of the curtain. It is most important that both curtain and lining are pre-shrunk as, though lining will seldom shrink, some curtains, especially linens, will. First cut off and join widths of curtains and of linings. Lay curtain flat with wrong side uppermost, turn under one selvedge and press. Lay lining over curtain with right side up, turn under matching selvedge and pin, tack and slip stitch together. Now from this row of stitching, measure approximately 30 cm./12 inches across the lining and place a row of pins through both thicknesses from top to bottom. Fold back the lining over the pins and work a row of loose, widely spaced buttonhole stitches along this line, making stitches about 5 cm./2 inches apart, and only taking one strand of the curtain fabric with each stitch. Replace lining over curtain and measure another 30 cm./12 inches across, pin, fold back lining and stitch in the same way. Continue right across curtain, then turn under remaining selvedge of curtain, press, turn under selvedge of lining and finish as first side. Now the lining is firmly attached. Turn over the top, sew on the tape and turn up the hem as given for unlined curtains.

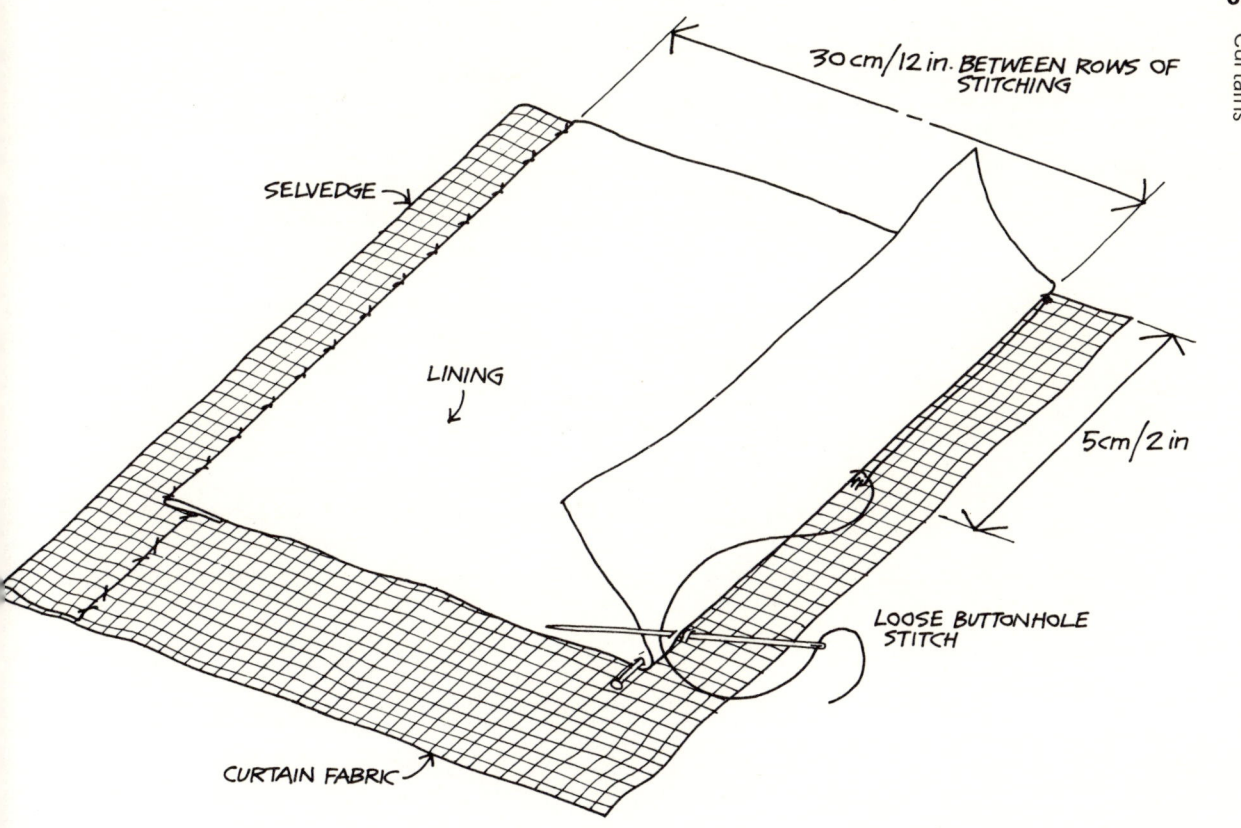

30 cm/12 in. BETWEEN ROWS OF STITCHING

SELVEDGE

LINING

5cm/2 in

LOOSE BUTTONHOLE STITCH

CURTAIN FABRIC

Altering the Length

This kind of alteration can very often be carried out successfully, but, as with altering garments, there is a snag if the curtaining contains any synthetic fibres. In this case it may have taken on a permanent crease along the fold line when the curtains were first made and pressed and no amount of pressing now will remove it. However this line can some- times be disguised by having a trimming such as braid or fringe sewn across it.

Shortening the length is a relatively easy job. Remember you have to take the same length off the lining too. First, determine just how much you want to take off the curtain, then unpick the original hem and the stitching along the selvedges (releasing the lining). Press work and cut off the unwanted length. Turn selvedges back under and press, then turn up hem again. Adjust lining by the same length. Don't be rushed into thinking that a machined hem is good enough as it's 'just an alteration'. The shorter the curtain the more obvious the hem is going to be. Finally slip stitch the lining back in place down the selvedges.

Lengthening curtains takes a little more time and trouble and needs more fabric too. Decide how much you want to add to the length and check whether you have sufficient matching fabric or whether a contrast or toning colour is going to be used, in which case make sure that it is of the same weight and, if possible, the same weave. Unpick the original hem and the stitching along the selvedges (releasing the lining) and press work.

If the amount you want to add is just the depth of the hem, then this depth is the amount you need to add, plus about 4 cm./1½ inches for turnings. With right sides facing, machine stitch one edge of the new piece to lower edge, taking 2 cm./¾ inch turnings. Press turnings downwards. Turn under selvedges and press. Fold under 2 cm./¾ inch along remaining edge and press. Fold added length in half and pin, tack and slip stitch in place along the line of machine stitching.

If a greater length is to be added, then again unpick the original hem and selvedges and press. Add sufficient material for the added length, plus the hem. Taking 2 cm./¾ inch turnings, machine stitch the extra length to the lower edge. Press seam opening. Turn under selvedges and press, then turn up the hem. The machine stitched line can be camouflaged with a bobble fringing or braid in a matching or toning shade sewn across it. Machine stitch this extra length to the lining too.

NET CURTAINS

Window Nets

These should measure at least twice the width of the window to look full enough; any less and they look mean. Mostly they are made of Terylene which is quite easy to sew, provided you use the correct materials. Synthetic sewing thread and ball pointed needles for either hand or machine sewing are essential, otherwise the work will snag and pucker suddenly — especially when machining. Keep all turnings to a minimum, otherwise they will tend to look heavy and clumsy as the light shines through them. Most Terylene net will not fray, so it's quite safe to snip the turnings close. There are one or two ways of buying and/or making nets.

Buying Ready-Made

These come in a variety of widths and lengths (often referred to as the 'drop' of the curtain). These range from 90 cm./36 inches to 204 cm./ 80 inches in length (the drop) by 90 cm./36 inches to 420 cm./168 inches in width. These ready-made curtains have the slot along the top for the curtain wire.

Buying Ready-Made and Finishing Them

You can also buy this type of curtaining by the metre; the width it comes in forms the drop and the length you buy determines the width. Again, this curtaining has the slot ready finished. When you have cut the various widths needed, you will find that with a lot of patterns and weaves, the ends do not have to be finished, they can just be cut very straight and left. The more finely woven ones though will need to have a very narrow hem along the sides. These can be hand or machine stitched.

Making Them Completely

If you need to make curtains for a variety of window sizes and you want them all to match, then buying ordinary unfinished net by the metre is best. In this case you *make* the curtain entirely. Cut the lengths as for ordinary curtains, allowing 5 cm./2 inches at the top to make the slotted heading, plus sufficient for the hem, remembering that the turning at the top of the hem must be kept very narrow. Selvedges do not have to be finished as they are usually very unobtrusive. However, if you have cut your own width and you have one raw edge, this ought to have a narrow hem in order to look balanced.

For the slotted heading, fold over 5 mm./¼ inch at the top and press, then fold over 4.5 cm./1¾ inches and pin, tack and machine stitch at the turned under edge. Make another row of machine stitching

2 cm./¾ inch from fold. For the hem, turn over 5 mm./¼ inch and press, then turn up remainder of hem and pin and tack, then this too can be machine stitched.

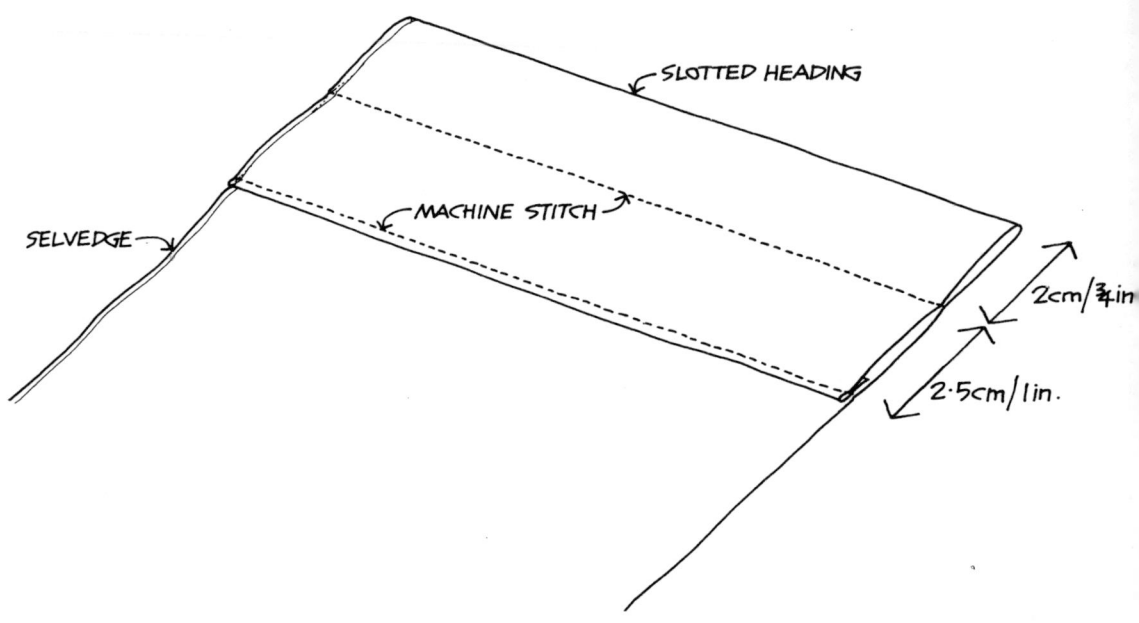

Floor Length Curtains or Nets

Curtains to be hung at doors or used as room dividers can be a very different proposition. Often they are made of loosely woven, coarse net and need to be treated carefully. To begin with there are lots of different fibres used in their manufacture. Terylene is the most straightforward and easiest to cope with. Very often they are a mixture of natural and synthetic fibres, ranging from Courtelle and Dacron to cotton, linen and even silk. Because of this they have a tendency to shrink when first they are washed, so do buy extra to allow for this. The shrinkage can be as much as 30 cm./12 inches on a door length. Usually they are made to hang from a curtain track, so make them as given for unlined curtains, using a similar sort of tape at the top, but made of nylon. To cope with the extra length allowed for shrinkage, make a deep, doubled, temporary hem *but do not press it*. After washing, the hem can be unpicked and re-sewn, adjusting the length as required. Even if there is not as much shrinkage as at first thought, the extra can still be trimmed off. It's better to be safe than sorry.

Even though this type of curtain is quite full and has a good length of drop, it will sometimes need a little help in hanging well. For this you can buy leaded weight in a long tube. Bought by the metre, it is slipped through the hem and lies along the folded edge to give added weight.

CUSHIONS

Cushions are really very easy to make, and to have lots of them — all in different colours and materials — lying around is sheer luxury. Most kinds of fabric can be used — satin, velvet, brocade and even pure silk. You can use different materials for each side of the cushion, so small pieces of material and oddments will do — small pieces can be joined to make patchwork, either traditional or in small squares machined together.

You will need a selection of fabrics. Bearing in mind your colour scheme, make a collection of them. Watch the remnant counters in furnishing departments of the large stores where real bargains in short lengths of fabric can often be found. Of course if you've made curtains of patterned fabric (see page 57), then you will already have these odd lengths and you can use them with great success mixed with toning fabrics. Look out for odd lengths of ruching, braid and fringing if you want to add this sort of trimming to your cushions. All you need in addition to your fabric is a cushion pad and a zip for the back of the cover. The zip is just about the last thing to buy as, for the length of this, you are governed by the size of the cushion. Usually the length of the zip needs to be about 2 cm./¾ inches shorter than one side of the finished cover.

Cushion Pads
There are very good feather-filled ones available in the stores. Though they are very expensive to buy, they do last and never go flat, so can be considered a good investment — one will outlast several covers. However you can make your own a lot cheaper. The filling can be something like plastic foam clippings: very cheap to buy, but they will always have a lumpy feel to them. Old nylon tights or stockings just clipped haphazardly into tiny pieces make a good filler, though even this kind of filling will never have the softness and resilience of feather-filled pads. The fabric for the cover of a home-made pad needs to be firm and finely woven. Down-proof cambric is ideal, but oddments of curtain lining can be used.
Cut the two pieces of cambric 1 cm./½ inch larger all round than the finished size is to be. With right sides facing place the two pieces to-gether and pin, then tack around three sides and half-way along fourth side. Using a very small stitch and taking 1 cm./½ inch turnings, machine stitch around the tacked area. Turn to right side and add the filling generously. With the turnings of the opening now folded inwards, close it by machine stitching the sides together just inside the folded edge. The cushion pad is the maximum size the finished cushion will be, but the cushion pad can be slightly *larger* than the finished cushion — this ensures that the corners of the cushion are well filled out.

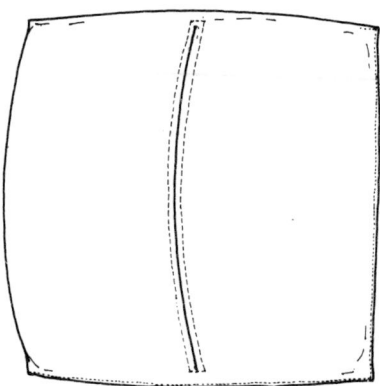

Plain Cushion Cover

You will need a piece of fabric 1 cm./½ inch larger all round than the finished size is to be (which should be slightly smaller than the cushion pad) plus two pieces for the back (each of these pieces to be half the size of the front plus 1 cm./½ inch more in width); zip fastener 2 cm./ ¾ inch shorter than finished size.

Sewing: taking 1 cm./½ inch turnings, join the two pieces of back together for 2 cm./¾ inch at each end. Using slot method, insert zip (see page 41) into opening. The back should now be the same size as the front. Having first undone the zip for about 2.5 cm./1 inch, place the back and front together with right sides inside. Pin, then tack them together, then taking 1 cm./½ inch turnings, machine stitch around outer edge. Snip across the seam allowance at each corner diagonally to remove some of the bulk of fabric. You can now completely unfasten the zip, which will enable you to turn the cover to right side. Ease out corners with the point of a needle so that they are squared. Finally, insert cushion pad.

Patchwork Cushion Cover

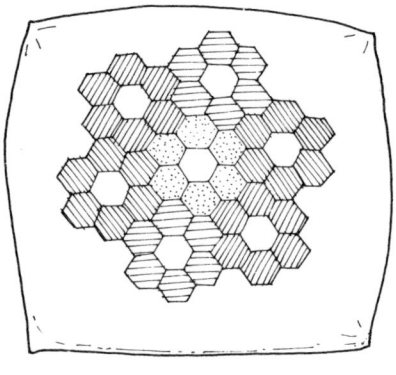

You will need fabric for front and back as given for plain cushion; oddments of cotton fabric for patchwork (each piece to be at least 5 mm./ ¼ inch larger all round than the actual size of hexagon given); zip fastener 2 cm./¾ inch shorter than finished size.

The patchwork is worked separately and then sewn to the front of the cushion before making the cover. First trace off the hexagon shape and, using this as a pattern, cut out a number of them in firm paper. To cover each shape, pin the paper on to the wrong side of the fabric with a single pin. Leaving 5 mm./¼ inch all round for turning, cut out. Fold the turnings over to wrong side and tack down through the paper shape, removing the pin as you work. For each flower you will need 6 hexagons in one colour with one plain one in contrast for the flower centre.

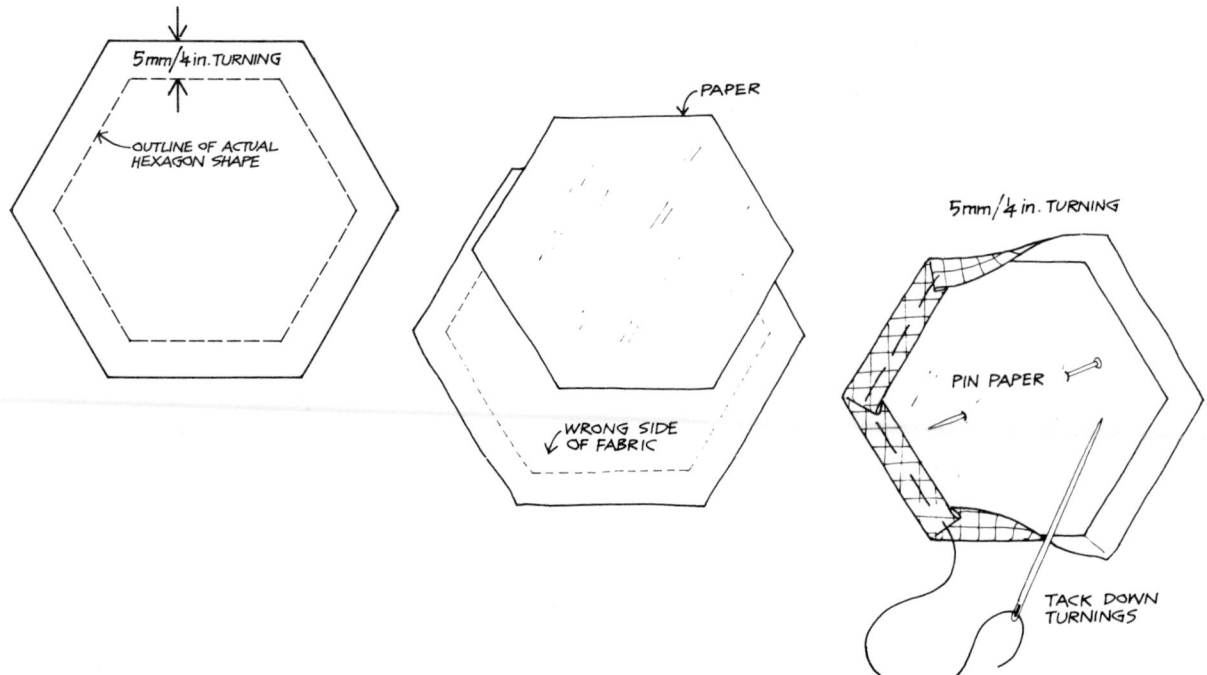

Each group of 6 hexagons is sewn together around the centre one. Sew each edge separately and to make sure that the stitching does not come undone, start just inside one end, work to the end, then turn and work back over these stitches to the other end, turn and work back for a few stitches before fastening off. With right sides of two hexagons together, make a small straight stitch through both thicknesses from back to front; take the thread diagonally over to the back and make another small straight stitch straight through to the front. This way the stitches will be inconspicuous on the right side.

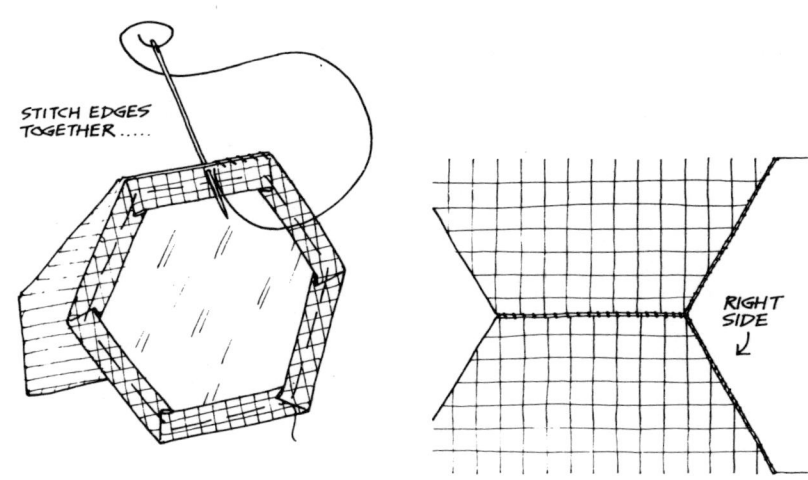

STITCH EDGES TOGETHER .....

RIGHT SIDE

When you have made several 7-hexagon flowers (6 or 7), sew them together in the same way to form an irregular shape. Press patchwork and remove tackings and papers. Lay the patchwork over the centre of the cushion front and pin, then tack in place. With very tiny stitches, hem all round.

To finish, join two pieces of back, insert zip and complete as for plain cushion.

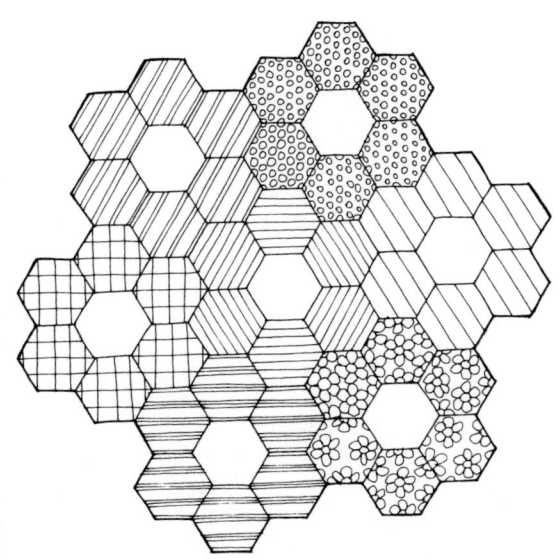

IT'LL BE NICE WHEN IT'S FINISHED....

HOME SWEET HOME

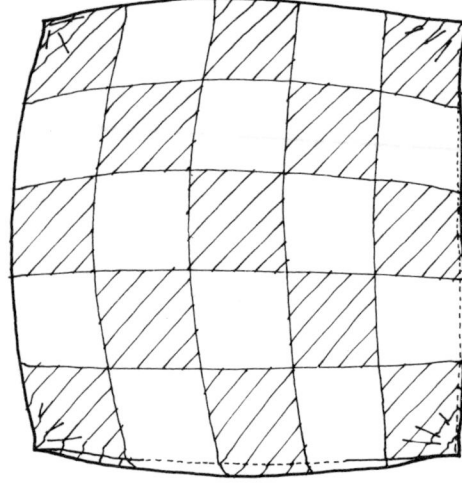

Machined Patchwork Cushion Cover

You will need a selection of fabric oddments all the same weight and
each one at least 10 cm./4 inches square; fabric for back as for plain
cushion and zip fastener 2 cm./¾ inch shorter than finished size.
Sewing: cut fabrics into 10 cm./4 inch squares, making sure that each
one lies straight to the grain of the fabric. Arrange them to form a
square. Pin and tack each vertical line of squares together to form long
strips. Taking 5 mm./¼ inch turnings, machine stitch them together.
Press seams open. Now pin, tack and machine stitch these strips
together in the same way to complete the square. Press seams open.

To finish, join the two pieces of back, insert zip and complete as
for plain cushion.

For a slightly different look, make a cushion that is almost the
same as the one above but as you place the strips together, add another
square to every alternate strip and you can then stagger the squares as
you join the strips by placing each seam of these strips to the centre of
the squares of the adjacent strip. By doing this, you will find you need
to trim off half a square at each end of alternate strips in order to
complete your square.

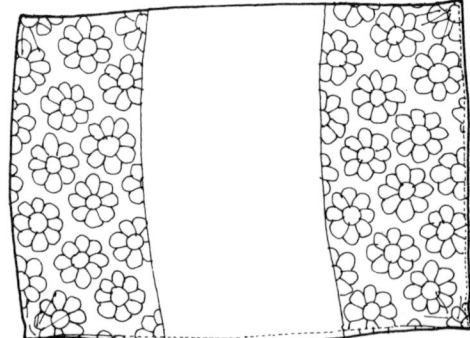

Oblong Cushion Cover

You will need three pieces of fabric for the front — of these, two pieces
should be matching plain or print and one piece in contrast (for centre);
each piece must be 2 cm./¾ inch wider than one third of the whole
width and 2 cm./¾ inch longer; two pieces of fabric for the back and a
zip as given for plain cushion cover; narrow flat braid to sew over seams
of cushion front (optional).
Sewing: pin and tack the three pieces of front together. Taking 1 cm./
½ inch turnings, machine stitch these seams and press open. If required,
on right side, pin and tack braid over these seams, then machine stitch
down each side of the braid.

To finish, join two pieces of back, insert zip and complete as for
plain cushion.

LOOSE
COVERS AND
UPHOLSTERY

Though making loose covers and re-upholstering furniture is usually
a job for experts, there is no reason why you should not tackle a simple
job of this nature yourself at home. A chair that needs the seat re-
upholstered and/or re-covered, or even just a simple stool top, can quite
easily be carried out by a beginner, and loose covers should be within
your capabilities.

BOX PLEAT

Loose Covers

Use very closely woven, hardwearing fabric such as plain or printed
linen, repp, velvet or velvet-type fabric such as Dralon if possible, as
these fabrics will hold their shape and will not look too crumpled after
they have been sat on a few times. Extra fabric will probably be needed
for velvet, Dralon or any fabric with a definite pile or nap, for, as with
curtains, the pile must always lie in the same direction. For a printed
fabric, you will also need extra fabric in order to centralize the pattern
on the seat or chair back. Bear these facts in mind when measuring, so
as not to buy too much in excess. Also, allow turnings of at least 2 cm./
¾ inch on all edges. You will also need twist pins and upholstery pins
for holding the sections in place.

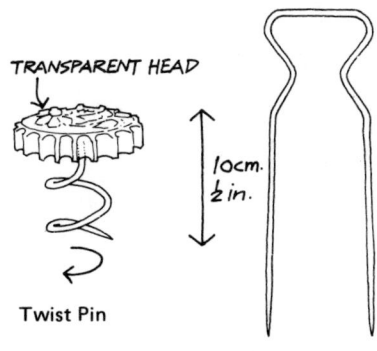

TRANSPARENT HEAD

10cm.
½ in.

Twist Pin

Upholstery Pin

Cutting out

Ideally the fabric should be pinned directly on to the chair or stool,
using upholstery pins, and then cut out; but this is probably too
ambitious, and I suggest you tackle the job in the simplest way. If you
are removing an old loose cover, unpick the seams and use the pieces as
a pattern. Otherwise, use an old sheet or a length of firmly woven cheap

fabric (such as calico) instead of the real fabric and pin this on to the chair or stool. In which case, remember to allow for turnings and cut out a pattern in sheeting. Pin the pattern on to the fabric and cut out. Where possible, pin, then tack the shapes together very securely and keep fitting the pieces on to the chair or stool as you go. When you are satisfied with the fit, you can then machine stitch the pieces together (again, check the fit as you work).

If the cover needs 'holding' in one or two odd corners, this is where the twist pins come in. Twist them through the fabric and into the upholstery; their transparent heads make them very unobtrusive.

If the lower edge needs a finish, you can add a border of box pleating. For this you will need a long strip of the matching fabric about 3 times the total length around the lower edge. As the final depth should be 12 to 13 cm./5 inches, on to this add the turning for it to be sewn on and sufficient for a machine stitched hem along lower edge (about 3 cm./1¼ inches). For this hem, turn under 5 mm./¼ inch and press, then fold over 2.5 cm./1 inch, pin, tack and machine stitch. To box pleat, fold fabric as shown, making each fold about 5 cm./2 inches deep and each box pleat measuring 10 cm./4 inches across. Place the central pleat to centre of front and firstly pin in place adjusting pleats very slightly towards corners, so that they all match with a whole pleat at each end.

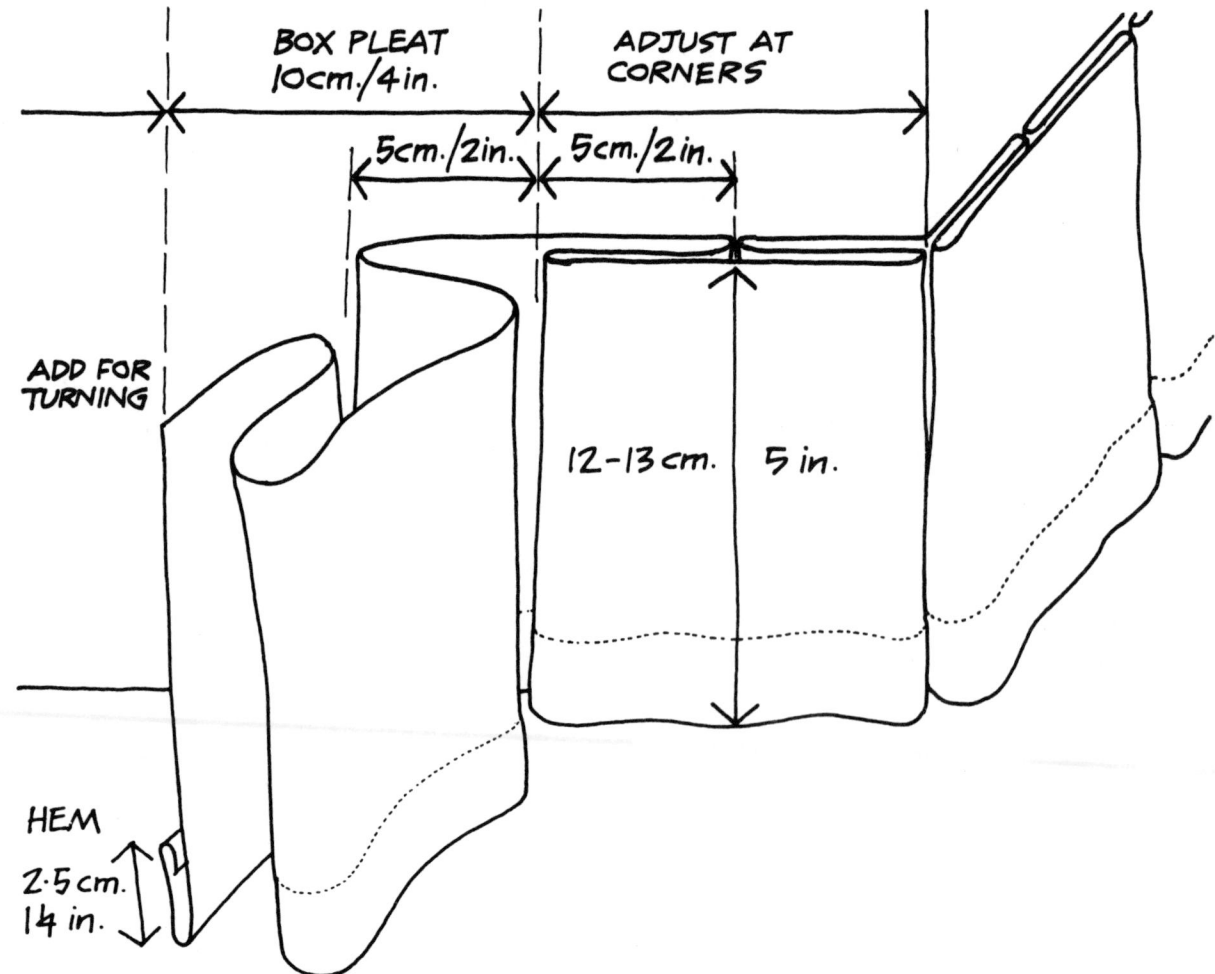

BOX PLEAT 10cm./4in.

ADJUST AT CORNERS

5cm./2in. 5cm./2in.

ADD FOR TURNING

12–13 cm. 5 in.

HEM
2·5 cm.
1¼ in.

Upholstery

A little more work is entailed here. Not only does it mean re-covering, but also replacing the padding (or filling) and maybe even the webbing at the base. Specialist shops sell all that is required in the way of padding, webbing and upholstery tacks. Haberdashery and soft furnishing departments also sell a limited range of small upholstery needs — canvas webbing, Copydex, strong waxed thread and the heavy duty needles including curved sail-maker's needles that you will need.

Taking it Apart

Carefully remove the original cover. If you can keep this all in one piece, so much the better, it can be used as a pattern when cutting the new cover. Next, carefully remove the old padding — it might be re-usable. Now you are down to the webbing.

Putting it Together

Check that the webbing is intact and strong. If not, it will have to be replaced. As you remove it, take note of how it was done. For a small stool, canvas webbing is probably strong enough, but for a chair, use rubberized (Pirelli) webbing. Though very tough to work with, it is much stronger and will therefore last.

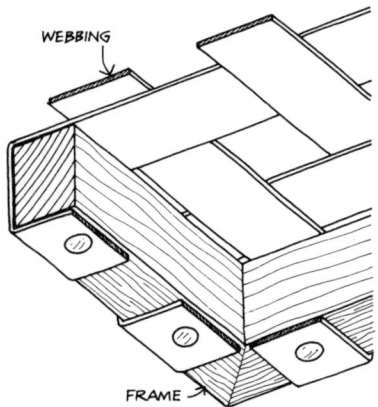

    The webbing should be woven over the seat and hammered to the struts with upholstery tacks. Leave a small space between the weave, and, for added strength, try if possible to wrap the webbing round to the outer side of each strut before securing it. If rubberized webbing is used, it will need stretching as you work and the going will be tough.

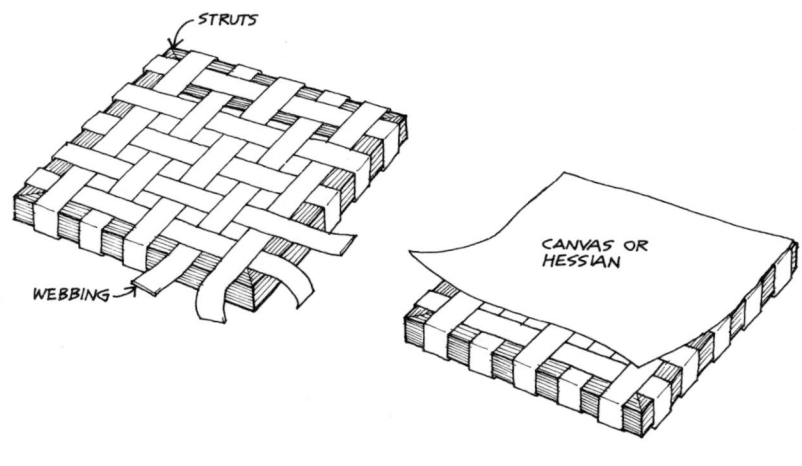

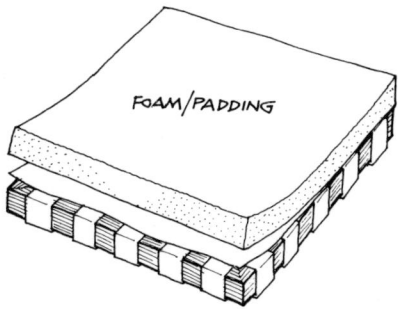

    Lay a piece of canvas or hessian over the webbing and, if it is at all re-usable, replace the old padding and if necessary add to it by building up the centre. For this, a piece of foam a little larger than the area to be padded is needed (the thickness will depend on the depth to be built up, but allow plenty). Taper off the outer edges to nothing, so that it lies almost flat over the centre. If the padding needs to be completely replaced, then buy a slightly larger piece of foam padding than the actual size you require. As it is covered tightly and firmly, it will contract into the cover and so have a well padded look with all corners well filled out.

Now for the outer cover. If it is to be fitted over the struts, you will need more upholstery tacks, but before doing anything, make sure that the fabric you are going to use will not fray or pull away. The best way of doing this is to spread Copydex all round the outer edges and leave it to dry. You can do this after you have cut your shape, but better still do it before, following the outline of the pattern. The fabric can then be cut through and will never fray or pull. If the re-upholstered seat does not sit in a frame a neat fold at each corner might be needed. The outer edges can be finished with a fringe or braid. This is usually sewn on using a curved sail-maker's needle, or, if it is not ot have any heavy wear, it can be stuck on with Copydex.

A Boxed Cushion

This is a very easy way of re-covering a loose chair seat or back-of-chair. First buy your boxed foam cushion shape, slightly larger than the finished size required.

You will also need: a piece of fabric which is twice the sum of the cushion length plus depth, by the sum of the width plus depth (for example, if you have a 50 cm./20 inch cushion shape 10 cm./4 inches deep, then you need a piece of fabric 120 cm./48 inches long by 60 cm./24 inches wide). By measuring and cutting the fabric exactly to the shape and then taking 2 cm./¾ inch turnings, the cushion shape will fit very tightly into the smaller area: Button thread: Machine needles size 100: Zip fastener 14 cm./6 inches shorter than one side.

To make: with right sides facing, fold strip of fabric in half across the width. Machine stitch short edges together for 2 cm./¾ inch at each end. Turn to right side and sew zip into remainder of opening using slot method (see page 41). Undo zip for about 2.5 cm./1 inch.

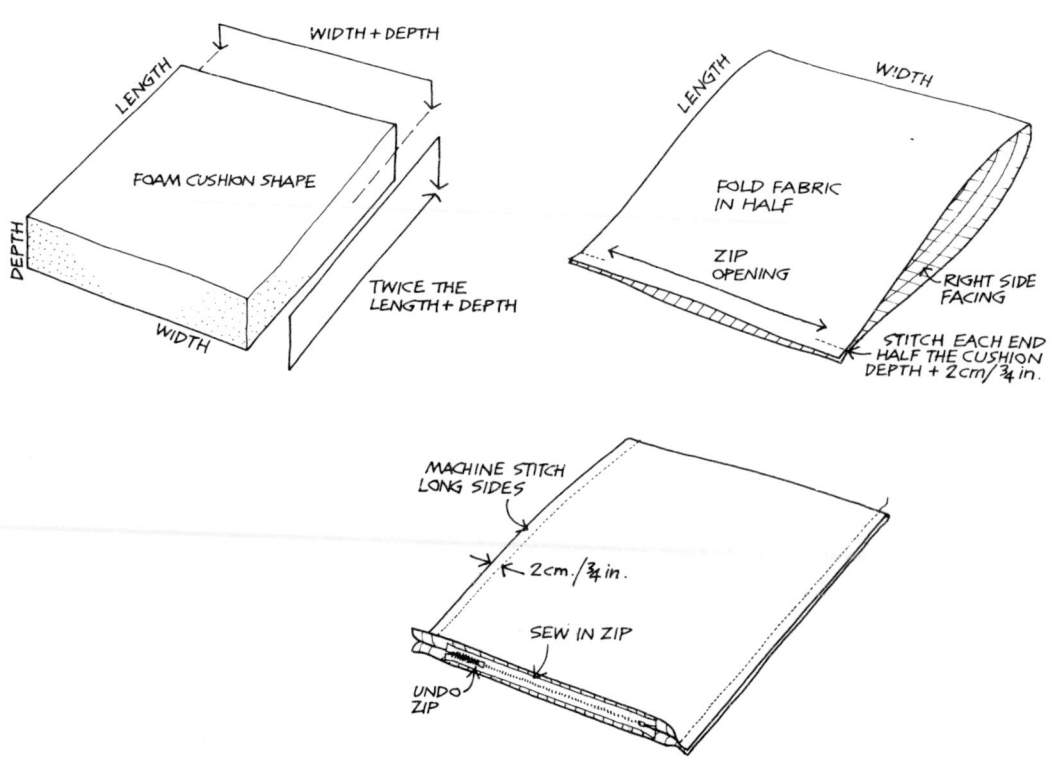

WIDTH + DEPTH

LENGTH

FOAM CUSHION SHAPE

DEPTH

WIDTH

TWICE THE LENGTH + DEPTH

LENGTH

WIDTH

FOLD FABRIC IN HALF

ZIP OPENING

RIGHT SIDE FACING

STITCH EACH END HALF THE CUSHION DEPTH + 2cm/¾ in.

MACHINE STITCH LONG SIDES

2cm./¾ in.

SEW IN ZIP

UNDO ZIP

Turn back to wrong side and join the long side edges. Now fold each corner into a triangular shape with a seam at the centre. Mark off each side of the centre seam to a depth of slightly less than half the cushion depth. Mark this measurement very carefully by tacking across and make sure that all four corners match exactly before you machine stitch. Trim off excess and neaten. Unfasten remainder of zip; turn cover to right side and insert cushion. The more difficult this is, the tighter and better the fit will be.

FOLD EACH CORNER.....

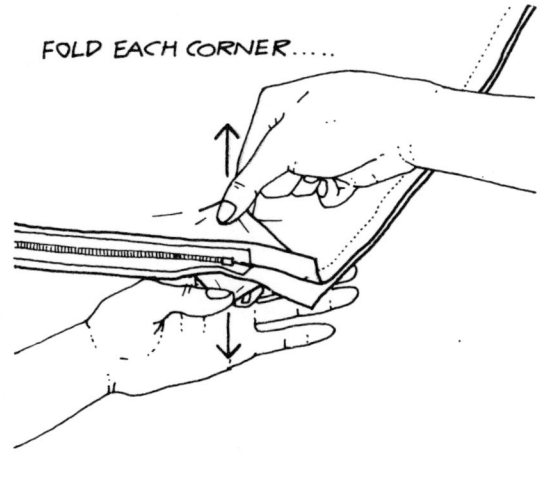

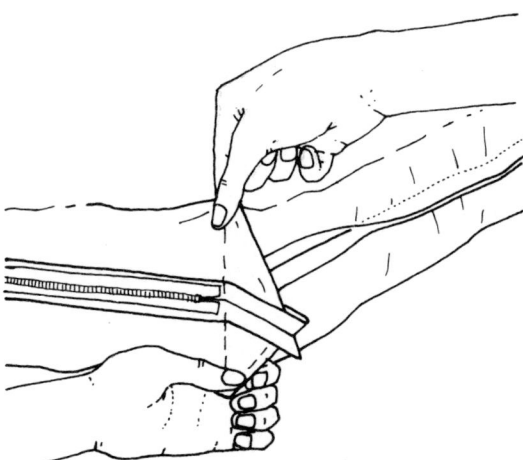

.....INTO A TRIANGULAR SHAPE

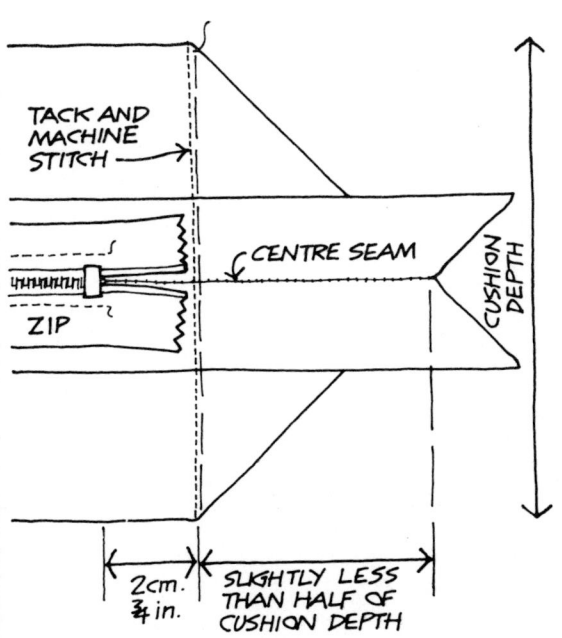

TACK AND MACHINE STITCH

CENTRE SEAM

CUSHION DEPTH

ZIP

2cm.
¾ in.

SLIGHTLY LESS THAN HALF OF CUSHION DEPTH

INSERT CUSHION

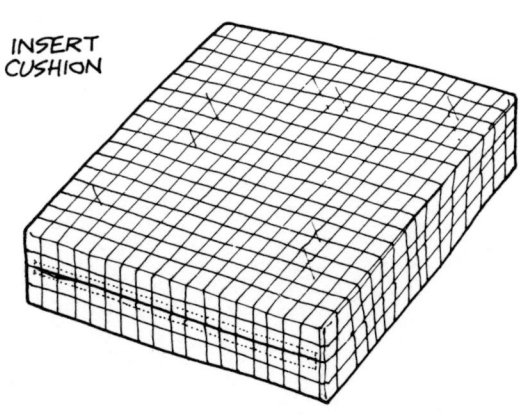

MAKES

Having now covered all aspects of what is often considered to be the dull side of sewing, you can now try your hand at simple dressmaking and make a complete garment from start to finish. Here are easy straightforward instructions for making a waistcoat and skirt (they could well team up in matching fabric), a bag and headscarf and, easiest of all, an apron.

How to Use These Patterns

Each square on the diagrams represents a 5 cm./2 inch square, so to get the intended size, each pattern piece has to be drawn on to paper marked out in 5 cm./2 inch squares (see Where to Buy).

Now using these grid lines as a guide, carefully draw the shapes on to the paper and cut out. Finally mark any symbols or instructions given in the diagram on to the pattern pieces.

Waistcoat in Two Sizes

81 cm./32 inch bust.
Length: 50 cm./20 inches

86 cm./34 inch bust
Length: 52 cm./20½ inches.

You will need: for either size, 1.20 m./48 inches of 90 cm./36 inch wide plain linen or linen-type fabric; for the lining, the same length of printed lawn or similar more finely woven fabric than that of outer fabric; matching thread; tailor's chalk.

For pattern: enlarge and cut out the two pattern pieces as given on page 84 in whichever size is required.

Cutting out: lay the pattern pieces *on the wrong side* of the linen. As you have cut a pattern for half the back and one front only, the two pieces must be cut out in doubled fabric; fold fabric with wrong side outside as shown on diagram. The straight edge of the centre back must lie right up to the folded edge; this edge is **not** cut.

To make sure the pattern lies perfectly straight on the fabric, measure from a vertical line of pattern grid at top of a piece and measure to the fold or selvedge; note the measurement and pin pattern down — measure again at base of same line to same edge and make sure that the measurement is the same as first one; pin.

You now know that the pattern is straight, so pin it down all round, then mark seam line all round with tailor's chalk. Add and mark a seam allowance of 2 cm./¾ inch on to outer edges of shoulders and

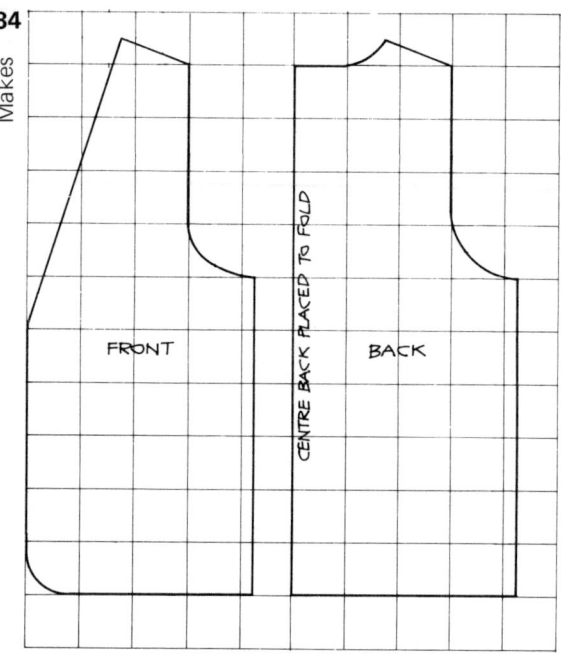

81 cm./32 inch bust

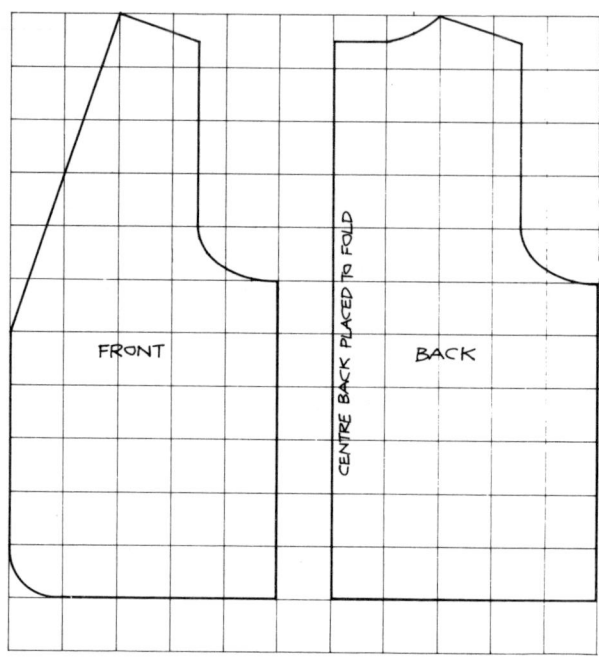

86 cm./34 inch bust

sides only. Cut out including these allowances. Remove pattern and place it on reverse side and mark all round with tailor's chalk as first side. Now cut out the lining in the same way. For the binding, the remaining lining fabric must be cut into 4 cm./1½ inch wide bias strips. To do this, cut the strips diagonally across the lining fabric as indicated on diagram.

Sewing: pin and tack shoulder and side seams of linen pieces, putting right sides together. Machine stitch. Remove tackings and press seams open. Join and press seams of lining in the same way. With wrong sides together place lining inside. Pin and tack all round the outer edge and armholes, 1 cm./½ inch from edge.

Taking 5 mm./¼ inch turnings, pin, tack, then machine stitch together the diagonal ends of strips into three lengths (see page 51) — one to fit round outer edge and one to fit each armhole. Remove tacking and press seams open. Beginning at centre back, place right side of binding to right side of waistcoat with edges together, and, taking 5 mm./¼ inch turnings, very carefully pin, then tack the binding in place, allowing a very little fullness at outer curves, but slightly stretching it around inner curves to ensure that it lies flat; join the ends at centre back in the same way as the lengths were joined. Machine stitch and remove tacking. Turning under 5 mm./¼ inch along remaining edge, fold binding in half to wrong side and pin and tack along stitching line. Stitch down and remove tacking. Beginning at underarms, finish armholes in the same way. Give a final press.

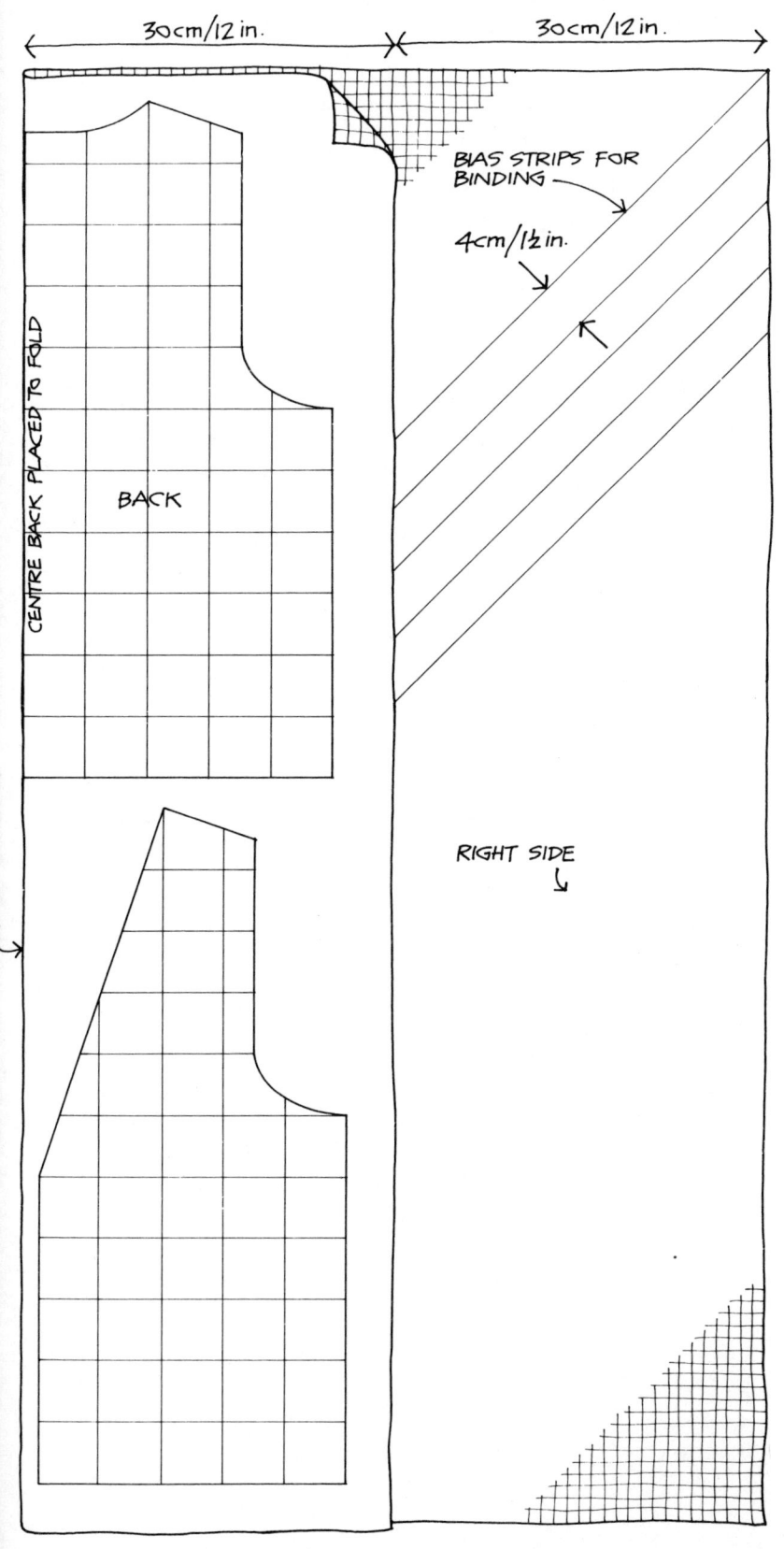

30cm/12 in.

30cm/12 in.

CENTRE BACK PLACED TO FOLD

BACK

BIAS STRIPS FOR BINDING

4cm/1½ in.

RIGHT SIDE

Makes

Gathered Skirt

Waist adjustable up to 76 cm./30 inches.
Length adjustable up to 71 cm./28 inches.

You will need: 1.50 m./1¾ yards of 90 cm./36 inch wide cotton fabric;
1 m./1 yard of 2.5 cm./1 inch wide waistband stiffening; 20 cm./7 inch
zip fastener; hooks and bars; matching thread.

Cutting Out: for waistband cut a strip the width of the fabric by 8 cm./
3 inches. For skirt, cut the remaining length in two.

Sewing: making sure that any pattern or 'way' of the fabric lies in the
same direction on both pieces, pin and tack the two pieces together
along the selvedges for side seams. Taking 2 cm./¾ inch turnings,
machine stitch these edges together, leaving a 22 cm./7¾ inch opening
at top of one seam for zip. Press seams open. Sew zip into opening by
the lapped method (see page 40).

 For gathers, work along each side of skirt separately from seam to
zip and vice versa thus: begin with a secure *Knot* in the gathering thread
and work a row of running stitches along 1 cm./½ inch from edge.
Leave an end and work another row 1 cm./½ inch below first row.
Holding the ends securely together, draw up this double row of stitching to half the required waist measurement. Secure the ends by winding
the ends in a figure of 8 fashion a few times around a pin placed
vertically through work.

 For waistband, start at left-hand side of zip opening and, with
right sides together, place band over skirt, with top of skirt and edge of
waistband together. Leaving 1 cm./½ inch of band extending for turning, pin, then tack band around waist, making sure that the stitches
run through the centre of gathering and leaving 4 cm./1½ inches
extending at right hand side of zip opening, 2.5 cm. for underwrap and
1 cm./½ inch for turning. (Do not remove pins holding gathering.)
Stitching through centre of gathering, machine stitch band to waist.
Now the gathers are secured, remove the pins. Enclosing stiffening to
within the 1 cm./½ inch turnings at each end, fold band over to wrong
side and folding under the turnings along band and at each end, slip
stitch in place.

 Fasten waistband with hooks and bars. Turn under hem. Remove
all tacking and press.

81 to 91 cm./32 to 36 inch bust
Length: 65 cm./26 inches
Sleeve length: 12.5 cm./5 inches

You will need: 1.50 m./1¾ yards of 90 cm./36 inch wide soft fabric
such as cotton lawn or fine Polyester; small matching button to fasten
back neck; matching thread; tailor's chalk.

For pattern: enlarge and cut out the two pattern pieces as given on page
89.

Cutting out: lay the pattern pieces on wrong side of fabric. As the
pattern is for half the back and front, this must be cut out in doubled
fabric both times. Fold the fabric down its length. The sleeves are cut
out once in doubled fabric. For the front, the straight centre edge is
placed to fold of fabric, but for the back, this edge is placed to the
doubled selvedge allowing 2 cm./¾ inch for centre back seam. Having
placed pattern pieces, pin them down all round, then mark all round
with tailor's chalk, after which mark a seam allowance of 2 cm./¾ inch
all round with a hem allowance of 4 cm./1½ inches at lower edge. Tack
a line through centre of sleeves as indicated, making very big, loose
stitches. Cut out remembering these allowances, and carefully snip
through tacking stitches. For belt, cut a strip the width of the fabric by
5 cm./2 inches. From remaining fabric cut bias strips (as shown on page
51) 4 cm./1½ inches wide for neck binding.

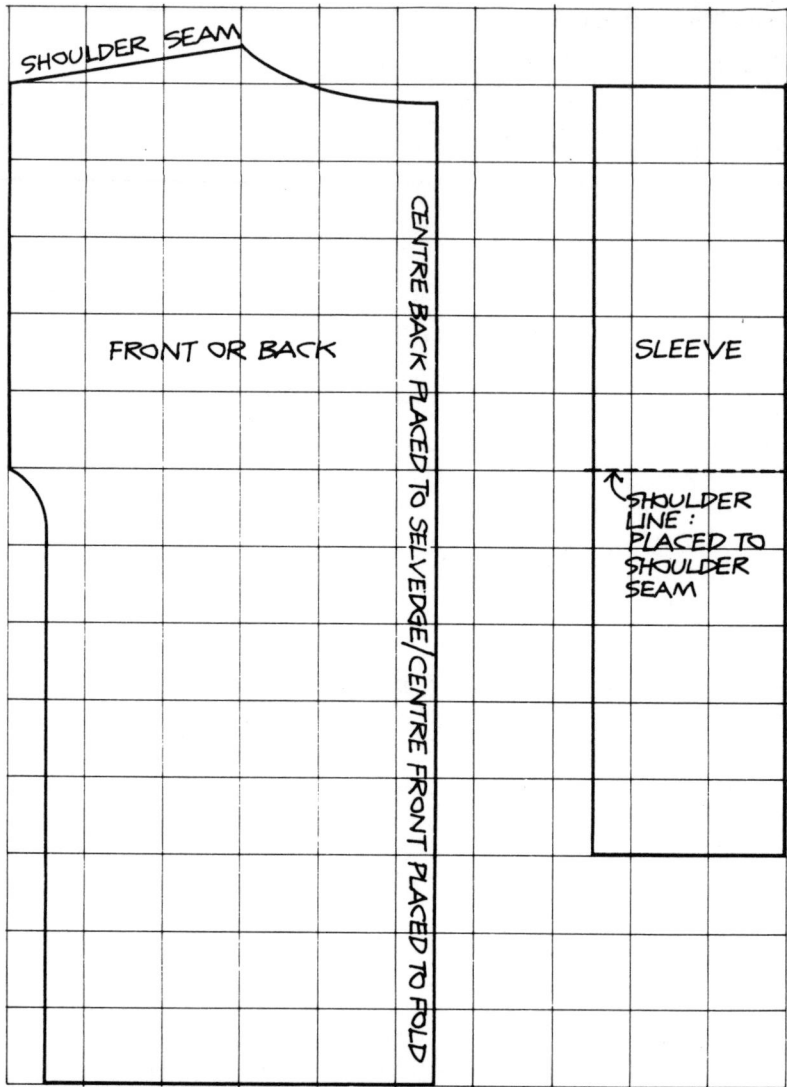

SHOULDER SEAM

FRONT OR BACK

CENTRE BACK PLACED TO SELVEDGE/CENTRE FRONT PLACED TO FOLD

SLEEVE

SHOULDER LINE : PLACED TO SHOULDER SEAM

Sewing: pressing seams open as you work, pin, tack and machine stitch centre back seam for 50 cm./20 inches from lower edge. Join shoulder seams in the same way. Setting tacked lines to shoulders, sew sleeves to side edges as shown, then join side and sleeve seams. Work another row of machining over first one just around underarm curve to strengthen it, then clip the seam allowance vertically down to the double stitching. This will ensure that it lies flat as you turn the work to right side. Turn under a narrow hem on sleeves and slip stitch down.

With centre back seam allowance pressed under, bind neck with the bias strips, joining them if required and turning under 5 mm./¼ inch at each end. Neaten ends with small slip stitches. For belt, fold strip in half along its length. Pin, then tack the long edge and one short end. Taking 5 mm./¼ inch turnings, machine stitch these edges. With the knob end of a knitting needle, push the short, secured end in, then continue to push it through until the whole belt is turned to right side. Press and neaten remaining end with small slip stitches. Remove all tackings. Buttonhole stitch a small loop to left side of back opening; sew on button to correspond. Press lightly.

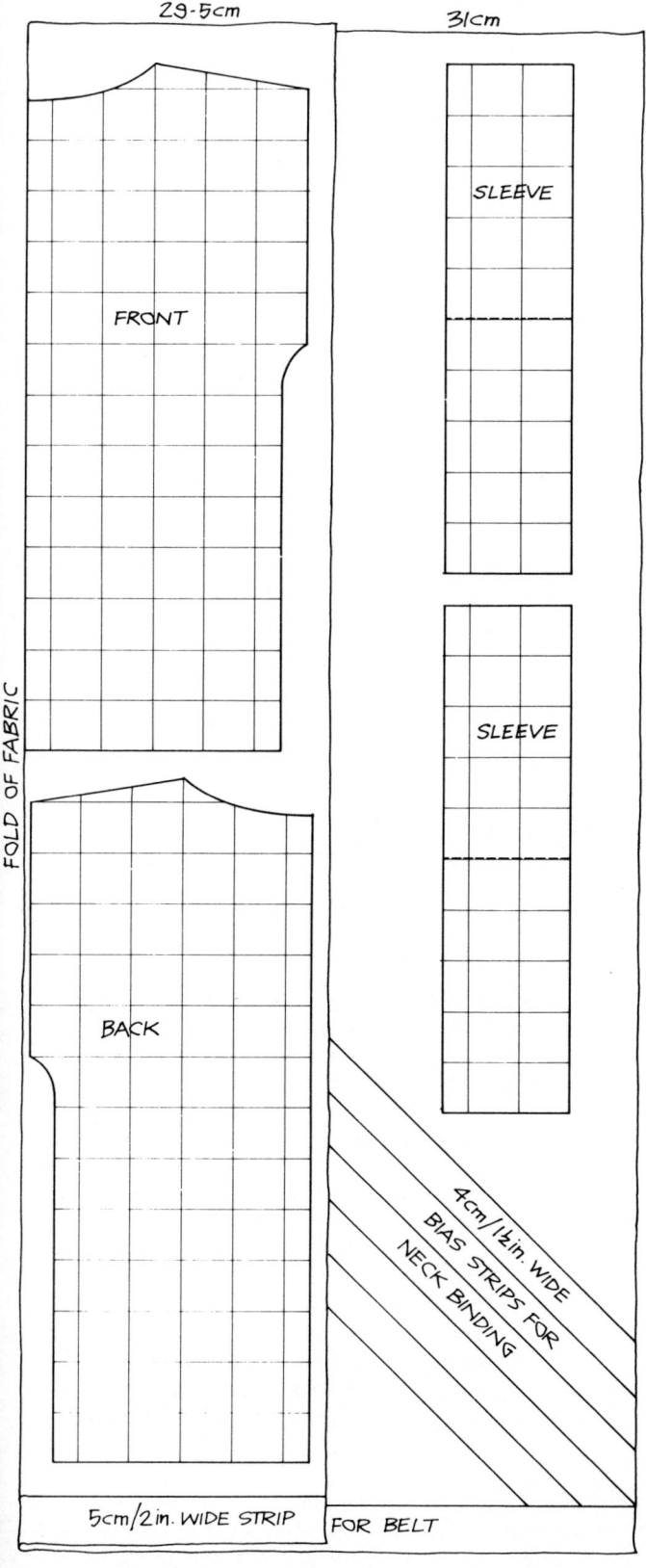

29·5cm

31cm

SLEEVE

FRONT

FOLD OF FABRIC

SLEEVE

BACK

4cm/1½in. WIDE
BIAS STRIPS FOR
NECK BINDING

5cm/2in. WIDE STRIP

FOR BELT

Apron

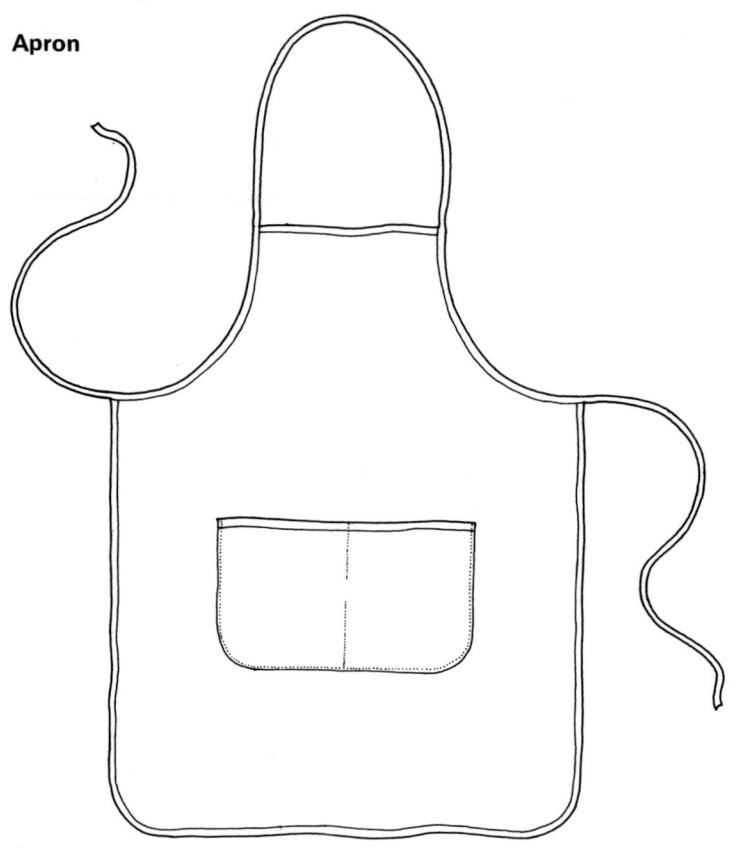

You will need: 1.15 m./1¼ yards of 90 cm./36 inch wide firm cotton fabric; two cards of bias binding; matching thread; tailor's chalk.

For pattern: enlarge and cut out the two pattern pieces as given on page 91.

Cutting out: Lay the pattern pieces on the *wrong side* of the fabric. As you have cut a pattern which gives only one half of the apron and pocket, you must cut out each piece in doubled fabric as shown. Fold the fabric in half along its length and lay the pattern pieces on to the fabric with the straight centre edges lying right up to the folded edge. Check that the pattern is straight in the same way as for the waistcoat. Pin down the pattern pieces.

First cut out the apron without any seam allowances at all, but do mark the position of the pocket (shown by dotted line) with long, loose tacking stitches. Now for the pocket, mark around curved edge with tailor's chalk, then on to this same edge mark a seam allowance of 5 mm./¼ inch. Remembering this seam allowance, cut out pocket without a seam allowance along the straight edge.

Remove pattern pieces, taking care not to pull out the tacking stitches, but just snipping through them, then as you unfold the apron you will need to snip through the tacking stitches again. This will still leave the pocket position clearly marked.

Sewing; first bind the short, straight top edge of apron, then all round lower curved section beginning at +. To do this, unfold one edge of the binding and lay this raw edge level with the edge of the fabric. Pin and

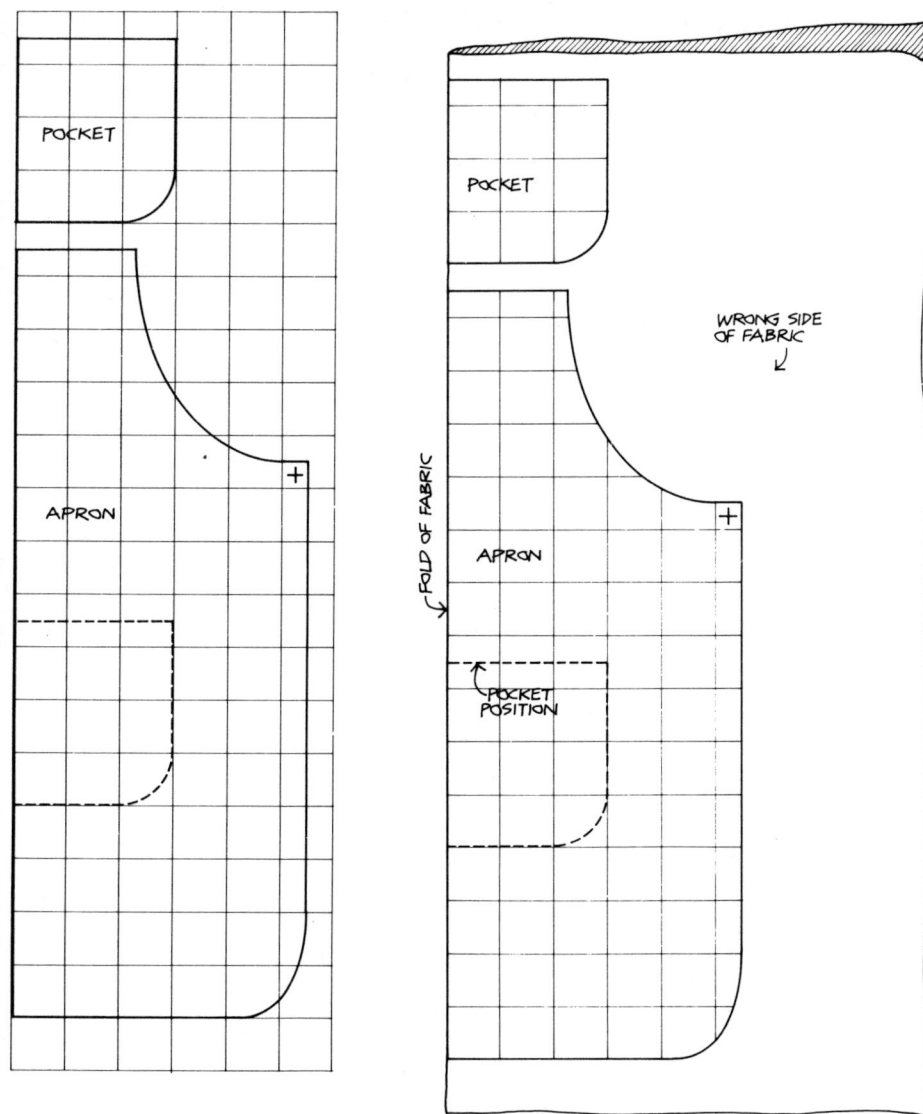

tack along the fold line, then machine stitch. Remove tacking and fold
binding in half to wrong side. Pin, tack, then hem the folded edge
along stitching line on wrong side.

Now begin again at right-hand side, and bind remaining curved
edges thus: leave 50 cm./20 inches extending (for one tie), pin and tack
binding along right-hand curved edge as given; do not cut off binding at
top, but first leaving a 56 cm./22 inch loop (for neck), pin and tack
binding along left-hand curved edge, finally leaving 50 cm./20 inches
(for 2nd tie) before cutting surplus. Turning in 5 mm./¼ inch at ends to
neaten them, complete binding as given, though for neck and ties the
folded edges of binding can be machined together. For pocket, turn
under the 5 mm./¼ inch turning, pin and tack in place. Taking 5 mm./
¼ inch turnings at each end, bind top of pocket. Place pocket on apron
as marked and pin then tack in position. Machine stitch down. Tack a
vertical line through centre of pocket, then machine stitch down this
line to divide pocket in two; fasten off ends securely. Remove all
tackings and press work.

Bag and Headscarf

Bag	**Headscarf**
50 cm./20 inches wide	81 cm./32 inches along head edge
40 cm./16 inches deep	40.5 cm./16 inches deep at centre

You will need: 120 cm./48 inches of firm sailcloth at least 90 cm./36 inches wide; for the lining and headscarf, 110 cm./44 inches of 114 cm./45 inch wide printed cotton lawn; matching thread.

The Bag

For pattern: enlarge and cut out the pattern as given on page 93.

Cutting Out: the pattern needs to be cut out in doubled fabric as shown in diagram. Lay pattern on *to wrong side* of the doubled fabric and make sure that it lies straight in the same way as for the waistcoat. Pin it down all round, mark the seam line with tailor's chalk, then add a seam allowance of 2 cm./¾ inch all round, and mark this. Cut out including the seam allowance. Mark the solid lines of darts and the fold line at the top by tacking through both thicknesses of fabric with double thread making big, very loose stitches. Carefully remove pattern, cutting through each tacking stitch as you do so and leaving the stitches in the fabric to denote darts and fold line. Now place the pattern on to reverse side and mark all round with tailor's chalk as for first side.

As you part the two pieces of the bag, again carefully snip through the tacking stitches still leaving darts and fold line marked.

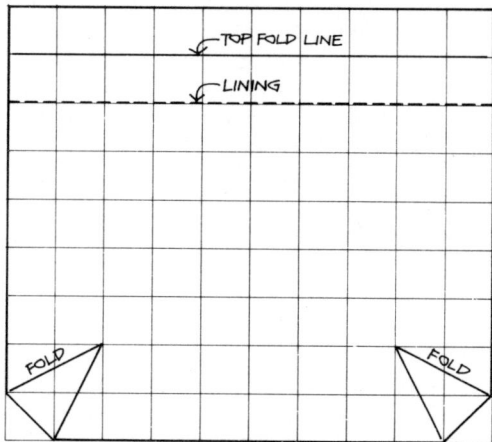

For lining, fold pattern at dotted line and cut lining from this pattern as given for outer bag (remembering to add the seam allowance at top).

For handles, cut two strips of sailcloth each 6.5 cm./2½ inches wide by 120 cm./48 inches long as given in diagram.

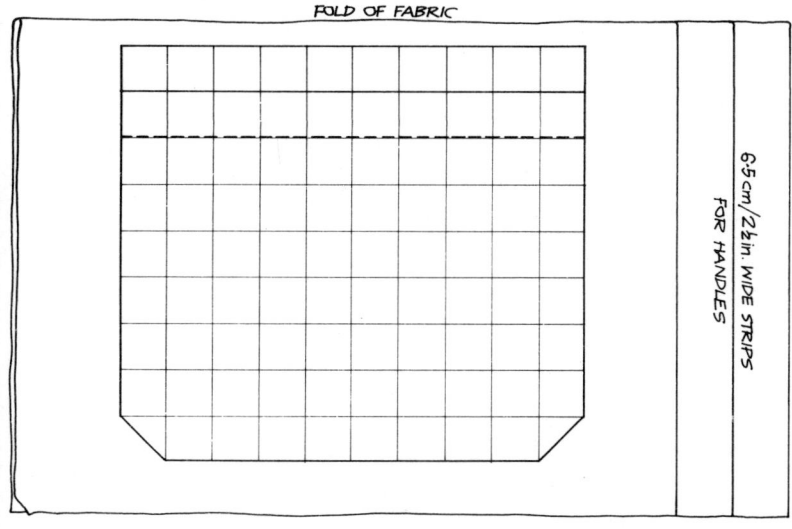

Sewing: for the outer bag, with wrong side facing, fold darts matching marking threads, and pin, then tack and finally machine stitch in place. Fold darts towards centre and press. Join two pieces of bag together, right sides facing, taking 2 cm./¾ inch turnings.

Join darts and the two sides of the lining together in the same way. **With right sides** together (placing one inside the other) sew the top edge of the bag to the top edge of the lining, leaving a 20 cm./8 inch opening along one side.

Turn the bag to the right side through this opening, then slip stitch the opening closed. Fold the top of the bag on fold line and press, then tack around 1 cm./½ inch from folded edge. Machine stitch around top, 5 mm./¼ inch from folded edge.

For handles, fold under 1 cm./½ inch along each long edge, tack, then press in place. Fold handles in half and tack down folded edges 5 mm./¼ inch from folded edges, then machine stitch these edges together. Machine stitch handles to top of bag about 13 cm./5 inches from seams.

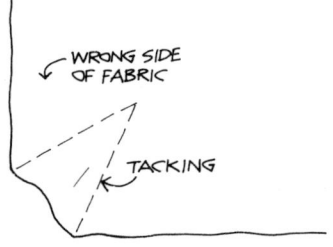

WRONG SIDE OF FABRIC

TACKING

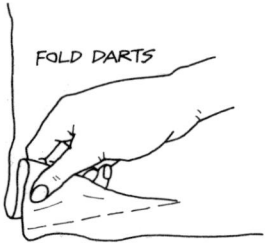

FOLD DARTS

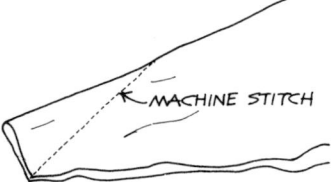

MACHINE STITCH

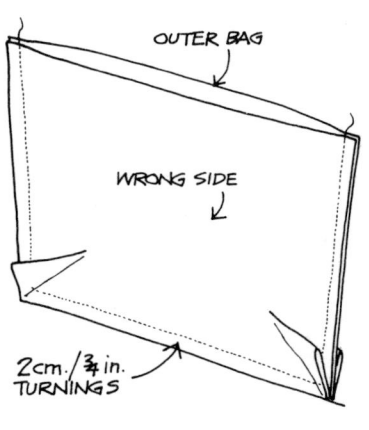

OUTER BAG

WRONG SIDE

2cm./¾ in. TURNINGS

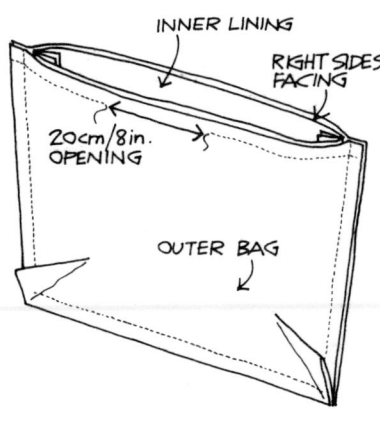

INNER LINING

RIGHT SIDES FACING

20cm/8in. OPENING

OUTER BAG

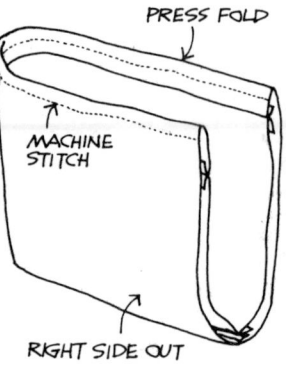

PRESS FOLD

MACHINE STITCH

RIGHT SIDE OUT

The Headscarf

Cut a 58 cm./23 inch square of fabric. With right side inside, fold it in half diagonally to form a triangle. Pin, then tack the edges together 1 cm./½ inch from edges, then, taking 5 mm./¼ inch turnings, machine stitch the edges, leaving a 10 cm./4 inch opening in one side.

    Remove tacking and turn the scarf to right side through the opening. Folding flat along seam line, ease out points of corners with the point of a needle. Press.

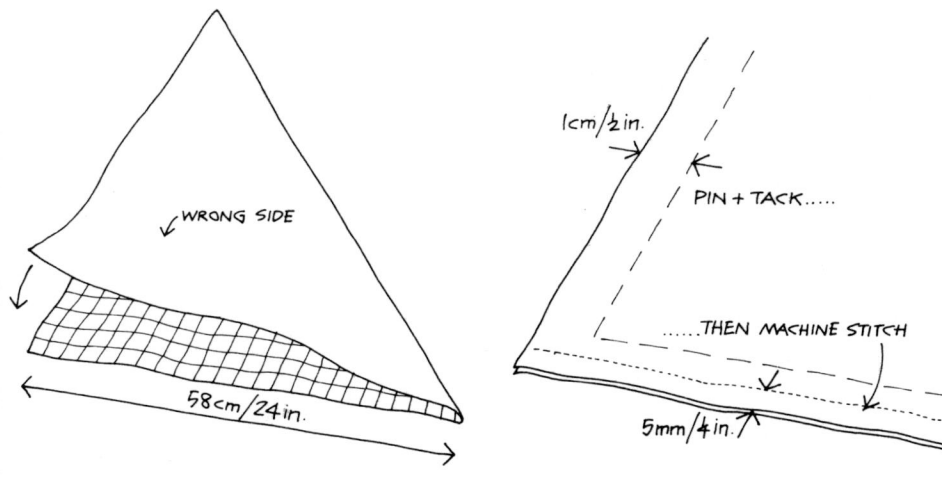

WHERE TO BUY

Most materials referred to in this book came from:
John Lewis
Oxford Street,
London W1A 1EX   Telephone 01-629 7711
Who supply all sewing accessories and a very wide range of dress and furnishing fabrics, interfacings, etc.

Upholstery
H. Burke,
80 Leather Lane,
London EC1
Will supply most upholstery needs, from pre-formed foam and latex foam cushion shapes, to Pirelli webbing, etc.

Pattern paper
R.D. Frank's Ltd,
Kent House,
Market Place,
London W1
Sell large sheets of pattern-cutting paper marked out in 5 cm./2 inch squares.